FIELDS FOR PRESIDENT

FIELDS

Illustrated with photographs

NEW YORK

FOR PRESIDENT

by W. C. Fields

Commentary and Photograph Selection

by MICHAEL M. TAYLOR

DODD, MEAD & COMPANY

Acknowledgment by W.C. Fields for Original Edition

Without the aid and suggestions and collaboration, the hammering and shoving of Charles D. Rice, Jr., this book would never have been written. If there are any complaints, please address them to Mr. Rice personally.

Acknowledgment is made to *This Week* for the portions of the text which ran in that magazine.

The Editor wishes to thank the following for their co-operation and assistance in the preparation of this volume: The Academy of Motion Picture Arts and Sciences, Hollywood, California; the special collections library of the University of California at Los Angeles; the film department of the Library of Congress; the movie history library of the University of Texas; the New York Library for the film at Lincoln Center; Mr. Donald Deschner; MCA Entertainment, Inc., for permission to use the many photographs from movies produced by Universal Pictures and Paramount Pictures; Metro-Goldwyn-Mayer; and finally Ilze Kupris who put up with my many moods through most of this.

M. M. T.

Contents

Introduction

TODAY W. C. Fields is considered one of the greatest of comic geniuses, although during his own lifetime he never received such just acclaim. He appears in movie houses, on television, in books, on records, posters, post cards, and sweatshirts. T.V. and radio, advertisers for an airline, a peanut company, and a coffee manufacturer have joined the rush to capitalize on the present recurrence in popularity of the pompous, cantankerous, blatantly larcenous, but endearing anti-hero—The Great W.C.

Part of the current Fields mania is that the Great Man is recognized as one of the original antiheroes so currently in vogue with today's "let it all hang out" generation. Despite the possible repercussions Fields uses his humor to kick society in the groin and with a fervor gratifying to all mankind. When he snarls at little brats, punches obnoxious inlaws, or outfoxes sly con men, he is rebelling against the impositions of an unreasonable society, hitting back in his own inimitable manner—right smack below the belt. And the gratified fans feel he is doing it on their behalf. Modern-day audiences are also more receptive to Field's brand of anti-establishment humor, because they tend to identify with and idolize this rasping misfit, aggressively at odds with society, who not only refuses to knuckle under, but brandishing his caustic wit, mounts an assault of his own.

From early childhood W. C. Fields showed that fanatical drive and dedication towards a goal, which separates the great from the mediocre and leads to success no matter what the chosen field. Although his formal education ended before he finished the fourth grade, he taught himself in the same determined manner which became the pattern for all he attempted:

"I thought of offering a young college graduate a trip (with him on a world tour) in exchange for teaching me. But after considerable thought, I decided it was cheaper to buy books. My reading matter started with a dictionary, next several different varieties of readers and books on grammatical construction. Then there were translations of Ovid and Virgil, then Dickens, Thackery, Shakespeare, Ben Jonson, Milton, Washington Irving, and Thomas Paine."

For many years after leaving home he lived virtually on the brink of starvation and at the mercy of the elements. At first dependent on friends to keep him in food and clothing, he was gradually forced to survive by his wits, pilfering from vegetable carts, Chinese laundries (where the language barrier made police protection difficult), butcher shops and from anyone who cared (or not) to help further the boy of destiny. But these were not idle years. It was about this time that Fields first became interested in juggling:

"I was 15 years old (other accounts place the age nearer 13) when the juggling urge first asserted itself. I was watching a vaudeville performance from the top of the gallery and the juggler came out to do his stuff. A glow came over me, a glow that still lingers in the famous Fields nose. I went out and started practicing and believe it or not, it was not long after that I managed to get a job juggling on the stage."

From then on most of his spare time was spent practicing this newly discovered art. Unlike other children of his age, while they played and slept, W. C. pursued his destiny.

"I still carry scars on my legs from those early attempts at juggling," he disclosed in a press release from *The Big Broadcast of 1938.* "I'd balance a stick on my toe, toss it into the air, and try to catch it again on my toe. Hour by hour, the damned thing would bang against my shinbones. I'd work until tears were streaming down my face. But I kept on practicing, and bleeding, until I perfected the trick. I don't believe that Mozart, Liszt, Paderewski, or Kreisler ever worked any harder than I did."

His determination, combined with his more than marginal skills, soon bore fruit, but as his success as a juggler grew, Fields' act began to undergo a change. It became more dependent on comedy for its appeal:

"You see, although my specialty was juggling, I used it only as a means to an end. I didn't just stand up tossing balls, knives, plates and clubs. I invented little acts, which would seem like episodes out of real life; and I used my juggling to furnish the comedy element. Somehow, even though I was only a kid, I had sense enough to know that I must work with my mind and not just my hands. If I hadn't realized that, I'd be laid on the shelf today. People would be saying, 'Bill Fields? Oh yes, he used to be a juggler, didn't he?'"

From comic juggler, Fields moved to traveling road shows and a world tour, playing privately before King Edward VII and other crowned heads of Europe, all before he was 21. The legitimate stage and vaudeville were next, and a starring role in the *Ziegfeld Follies* from 1915 to 1922 followed.

Films came next. His excellent comic pantomime got him roles in silent pictures as early as 1915, but he explained it in a different way:

"As long as I did pantomime, the silent motion pictures wouldn't give me a tumble. But the moment I began to speak on the stage, I got an offer to go into silent films. Probably they wanted to keep me quiet."

After one or two supporting roles, he was signed with star billing to a three year contract with Paramount.

But he wasn't content to be "laid on the shelf" here either. When his contract expired, he left Paramount and the East, and together with all his worldly belongings (340 one thousand dollar bills pinned to the lining of his suit and three steamer trunks—one filled with clothes, the other two with booze), he headed for Hollywood.

When he reached Hollywood, he wasn't received with the great enthusiasm he had anticipated! "Talkies" were a whole new field with their own super stars, and the film moguls were not interested in taking a chance with a semipopular comic. They were interested only in the tried and proven greats—Greta Garbo, Wallace Beery, the Barrymores, etc. So for 18 months Fields roamed Hollywood searching in vain for a break. This was one of the hardest periods of his career. Old fears of hunger and poverty began to haunt him. He was constantly badgered with offers for stage roles and other comic spots, and he began to question the merits of his decision.

In a later press release he discussed that period:

"I was so broke that people were picking up stray pieces of Mr. Fields all over Hollywood and trying to put them together again. Unable to get work, I evolved a plan. I went to a certain studio—which will remain unnamed as I do not wish to embarrass them—and made a proposition. I had an idea for a film. I would direct it and act in it myself. And I would not ask a single morsel. All they had to do was put up the money, and a cheap two-reeler it would have been. I was confident that it would be successful and that they would hire me for more two-reelers.

"I thought it was a swell proposition, but they didn't. They turned it down flat. My, my. I'll bet their faces are red now!"

But his confidence held out and his chance finally came in 1930 when he made a two-reeler, *The Golf Specialist*, for R.K.O. From there his fortune was made. His pantomime along with his perfect voice, with its nasaled wheeze and implied highhandedness, combined to make him a film star from the beginnings of talkies to his death in 1946.

One of the most striking features of Fields' struggle to survive and succeed was the amount of deception and chicanery he fell victim to. Life is certainly bound to be hard for a young lad making his way through the world alone, but Fields suffered uncommonly harsh treatment. It was just this unique and sometimes tragic fight, however, which shaped the character of the man and influenced his attitudes and his portrayals on stage. And he drew heavily on these experiences from his hard fought youth as source material for his humor, quite possibly to get some personal revenge, with his most effective weapon, satire, on those who had taken advantage of him during his vulnerable years. It was in the beginning of his show business career when Fields was most abused (which accounts for his frequent characterization of the shady-roadshow-con man). The following is a quotation of his from a theater magazine.

"I got an engagement (his first) at a summer park, through a booking agent. I'll never forget the name. It was Flynn and Grant's Park, at Norristown, N. J., and it was a twenty-five cent trolley ride from Philadelphia. I was paid five dollars a week. I got the five dollars, but I had to pay a dollar and a half commission to the booking office (who was incidentally the show's manager) and it cost me over four dollars to ride back and forth to the park."

Fields felt that despite a loss of more than fifty cents per week, not to mention living expenses, the exposure was well worth it. To add insult to injury, at the end of the engagement Fields was docked two-weeks' salary by the unscrupulous manager as sort of a reversed severance fee! His next job was for ten dollars a week and "cakes" (meals).

"A favorite way to fill up the place was to work a fake rescue. One of the performers would go out in the surf, pretend to be caught in the undertow, and shout for help. We would all be ready, rush into the water, and drag the rescued person into the pavilion. Naturally, the crowd followed, and if it was a woman we rescued, the crowd was particularly large. Once inside they bought drinks, and we were supposed to be entertaining enough to keep them there."

Aside from the abundance of water (to which he later attributed his distaste for that beverage), another problem in this job was that although the negotiated wages were acceptable, they were frequently not collectable. Fields quickly left this grueling and unprofitable position for a better one.

"It was a one-night affair, owned by a man named Jim Fulton. Here was another step upward. I got twenty-five dollars a week, but it was rather precarious and some weeks we did not get our salaries."

Fields was soon promoted to one of Fulton's road show companies. The road manager, however, was as slippery a character as Fields ever portrayed later. He left the company stranded, running off with all the back salaries and Fields' total life savings which he had been lending to the fellow at a promised interest rate of fifty percent! ("Fifty percent interest was a cruel temptation," Fields remarked later, "especially for a lad of 16.")

In a press release from a movie he wrote and starred in, *The Old Fashioned Way* (Paramount, 1934), which like many of Fields' movies, is based on just such early encounters, he spoke of a typical experience with a "tank-town" sheriff:

"The sheriff and his partner were going to beat us up or vice versa. I hid in the coal tender of the train. The train pulled out just in time. Many times a drain pipe was the only means of ducking unpaid hotel bills.

"Yes, I've been through it all—even to dodging over-ripe tomatoes. The audiences' aim was remarkable. It's nice to be safe in a motion picture."

After many hard years of struggling, W. C. finally made it. But the impressions of life and people he had formed never left him, and he handed them right back to audiences whenever possible. In the characters he portrayed on stage W. C. Fields embodies his own personal solutions to life's obstacles. The man on stage and the man off stage were one and the same, which made his performances so much more believable and realistic. He is secure in the knowledge that, with a little bit of chicanery, victory will eventually be his. He is confident that one of his elaborate schemes is bound to pay off (as long as he can brazen and bluster his way through the temporary inconveniences). His only slight doubt is that when his ship inevitably does come in, he will be stranded at the railroad station.

When success ultimately comes to the Great Man, usually from some unanticipated and unlikely source, he receives his rewards with unquestioning confidence and nonchalance, as if it were all an inevitable part of his masterly scheme. He proceeds to wallow in the glory of his prevaricated success story, embellishing it further with each of the frequent recountings.

Finally, when he almost has us convinced, he slowly assumes that larcenously, confident leer, and as the camera fades, we sense his final uncompromising message to the world: "You can't cheat an honest man, never give a sucker an even break, or smarten up a chump."

W. C. Fields was not only an exceptional comedian, he was an excellent comedy writer. During his career, he wrote numerous short comic essays, newspaper articles (usually consisting of extremely one-sided reviews of his own act), and most of his material for vaudeville and the *Ziegfeld Follies.* Under assorted pen names, he wrote many of his motion pictures, some of which have become comedy classics of all times such as *It's a Gift* and *The Bank Dick.* And in 1939, he wrote *Fields for President,* his one and only book in which he takes the golden opportunity to settle, in the lasting medium of print, with many of the institutions and groups he found most offensive.

When the manuscript was originally published in 1940, it was only mildly successful, although today an original copy is a rare collector's item. The problem was that it was received as an ordinary book written by a novelist, which it definitely is not. It is an anthology of humorous gags, sketches, and comic situations laced together with a hint of a plot line, only for appearances. As Fields' stage humor was heightened by a well-timed concise delivery with many short throw aways and innuendoes lecherously rasped under his breath, his manuscript should be rendered in the same manner. To get the full effect of the humor, it should be read slowly and with all the nasaled asides which the Great Man would have used himself. Don't let paragraphs or sentences dictate the flow of the material. Follow the situations and punch lines themselves, and for the best results, mix vigorously with a quart of good gin.

MICHAEL M. TAYLOR

Chapter 1

"Let's Look at the Record"

Fields is imminently qualified for the post of the world's greatest comedian:

1. Tramp juggler and comic starting at age 15.
2. Played for the crowned heads of Europe before he was 21.
3. Starred in and wrote for the Ziegfeld Follies from 1915 until 1922.
4. Starred in the Broadway play Poppy in 1923 and 1924.
5. Began his silent film career in 1915 as the star of The Pool Sharks.
6. Starred in nine out of the ten silents in which he appeared between 1925 and 1928.
7. Appeared in twenty-nine motion pictures from 1930 to 1945, starring in more than half of them.
8. Wrote many of his motion pictures, some of which have become all-time comedy classics (Man on the Flying Trapeze and Never Give a Sucker an Even Break).
9. Performed on radio (Chase and Sanborn and Lucky Strike Hours), recorded for Columbia and Decca, and even wrote this book.

And so remember, my friends, a vote for Bill Fields is a vote for one of the greatest comic geniuses that ever lived.

Tramp juggler and distinguished comedian starting at age 15

"Responding to an automatic alarm signal, police appre-hended an unarmed marauder in Schmackpfeiffer's Cruller Works tonight."

Never Give a Sucker an Even Break (© 1941, Universal Pictures)

NO DOUBT most of my gentle readers were both amazed and delighted when the news of my candidacy for the chief office of this fair land blazed forth on the front pages from coast to coast. I remember one particularly colorful account in an important California daily:

LOS ANGELES MAN HELD IN
CRULLER-FACTORY BREAK

Los Angeles, March 25 (AP)—Responding to an automatic alarm signal, police apprehended an unarmed marauder in Schmackpfeiffer's Cruller Works tonight. The accused claimed that he had attended an Episcopal strawberry festival earlier in the evening and had lost his way home, ending up in the cruller factory by some strange twist. He gave his name as W. C. Fields, a comedian and a candidate for the Presidency in 1940. Officials expressed the belief that he might well be a Presidential candidate, since half the crackpots in the country were running, but they had serious doubts that he was a comedian.

It was one of the nicest police stations I've ever been in, too . . . but there! I must not digress into sweet memories. The matter at hand is this: Right off the bat I wish to dispel some of the vile rumors built up around me by my political adversaries. In the first place, I never stated that Buzzie Dall was a sarsparilla-drinking, cribbage-playing, evil old man. Nor did I ever declare that America's frontier was in France—though I know of a little hostel on the Boulevard Raspail that would make a delightful place for a frontier. And thirdly, never at any time have I promised the voters of America two chickens in every garage. The men who have spread these preposterous calumnies are merely my terrified political opponents.

The purpose of this modest little volume is to make clear to my future constituents what my moral and political background has been, and exactly how I stand on the issues of the day. So just pull up a fireside and lend an ear to your old Uncle Will, the white hope of the Bull Moose Party in 1940.

In the first place, many of you have asked why I am running for President when I already have a promising future as a veterinary (I've been studying nights). To this question I merely reply: "There's a reason for everything."

The reason Columbus discovered America was that he wished to find India. Abraham Lincoln liberated the slaves because he wanted to make all men free and equal. My cousin Haverstraw married a tattooed lady for art's sake alone.

However, the reason I am running for President is somewhat more complicated. It dates back to that fateful day when my first spark of interest in politics was

"The purpose of this modest little volume is to make clear to my future constituents what my moral and political background has been."

My Little Chickadee (© 1940, Universal Pictures)

fanned to a glowing ember. I was exactly nine years old, and I can remember clearly how Boss Tweed's brother, Harris Tweed, took me on his knee and said:

"Will, whatever you do in the years to come, always remember one thing: Never give a sucker an even break."

At the time, my youthful mind did not grasp the whole significance of this great precept. In fact, not until I was in my late twenties did the truth of it burst forth upon me in all its glory.

At that time I made a tour of the Southwestern states selling an amazing preparation called Raro Hair Restorer. I had obtained the formula from a beautiful Indian princess—Weeping Sinew, I believe was her name. One hot July day I sold a bottle to a baldheaded gentleman in Cowcatcher, New Mexico.

"Will this really work?" he asked.

"Squire," I returned in my inimitable manner, "this colossal medication will grow hair in a bathtub!"

The next day he returned and wanted his money back.

"What's the trouble?" I demanded. "Doesn't it do everything I said it would?"

"Oh, yes, it works all right," he said, "but I've decided I don't like hair in my bathtub—it tickles hell out of me."

From that day on "Never give a sucker an even break" has been my watchword, and my ideal has been to rise to the one great position in the nation where I

Two Flaming Youths (© 1927, Paramount Pictures)

"At that time I made a tour of the Southwestern states selling an amazing preparation called Raro Hair Restorer."

may exercise it to the fullest.

Ideals have always been a strong consideration with me, anyway. Just this past January I risked catching my death of pneumonia for an ideal. I was dining with a few political colleagues at the Mayflower in Washington. If memory serves me correctly, among the guests were Franklin and Eleanor Roosevelt, Cordell Hull, Harry Hopkins, Miss Frances Perkins, Chief Justice Hughes and Gypsy Rose Lee.

During the baked-flounder course, Secretary Hull leaned over to me and purred in a guileless tone: "Fields, would you care for the Worcestershire sauce?"

It was no more than a clumsy attempt to trick me into revealing my stand on naval appropriations.

"Sirrah!" I snapped, "my seconds will call in the morning!"

Whereupon I stalked from the dining room in high dudgeon, and it was not until I was out on the icy street that I realized I had no shoes on (I had slipped them off under the table before putting my feet in Miss Perkins's lap).

As a result I spent two weeks at the Ellin Speyer Memorial Hospital, but I did not rue my action. It proves what a man of my caliber will do for his principles.

I am truly a candidate with both feet on the ground. I take no fol-de-rol from any man, much less any fiddle-faddle. And when, on next November fifth, I am elected chief executive of this fair land, amidst thunderous cheering and shouting and throwing of babies out the window, I shall, my fellow citizens, offer no such empty panaceas as a New Deal, or an Old Deal, or even a Re-

"I am truly a candidate with both feet on the ground."

Never Give a Sucker an Even Break (© 1941, Universal Pictures)

Deal. No, my friends, the reliable old False Shuffle was good enough for my father and it's good enough for me.

Furthermore, I shall not mince words in my first message to Congress. Though full many a solon's cheek may flush with embarrassment, I shall point out these trenchant and oft-evaded issues:

1. Political baby-kissing must come to an end—unless the size and age of the babies be materially increased.

2. Sentiment or no sentiment, Dolly Madison's wash *must* be removed from the East Room.

3. What actually *did* become of that folding embrella I left in the Congressional Library three summers ago?

When, on the fourteenth of February last, I outlined my plan of action in a speech at Des Moines (the night some scoundrel Tory sneaked a snapping turtle into my water pitcher) political circles were set agog. "Who is this person who proposes to revolutionize our government?" they demanded. "Merely a presumptuous dark horse!" Some even went so far as to call me a certain part of a dark horse.

To refute these charges, right here I should like to review briefly the major incidents of my amazing career, for the benefit of any benighted reader who, like my Des Moines opponents, is not acquainted with the Fields Saga.

I was born in a humble log cabin a scant stone's throw from Grant's Tomb, the second son of a lowly cordwainer. (Father was one of the lowliest men I ever knew, measuring less than twelve feet on a pair of seven-foot stilts. He could stand on his head under the kitchen sink, but seldom did so, arguing that there was not much point to it in the first place.)

When Father was not busy waining cords, he worked as a substitute horse-car driver. One of my most vivid

"When father was not busy waining cords, he worked as a substitute horse-car driver."

(circa 1899. University of Texas)

recollections is driving with him on the day of the blizzard of '88. He had his horses frozen stiff right in front of Mr. Terrence O'Flanagan's saloon on Eighth Street. The conductor, a very dear friend of Dad's, succumbed to the sub-zero weather on the rear platform, his hands frozen tight to the change box. If it had not been for Father's miraculous presence of mind, there might have been dire tragedy that day. However, he immediately jumped from the car, ran up to O'Flanagan's saloon and opened the swinging doors wide. The fumes that poured out revived the horses in a trice. Snorting with excitement, they pulled the car right off the tracks and galloped into the barroom. The conductor thawed out, finished ringing up his fare and stepped over to the bar. Everyone had a Rock 'n Rye on Dad— except the two valiant steeds, who, obviously, were already supplied with horse's necks.

Of course, I have other early recollections—but perhaps my dear readers would obtain a more colorful idea of my youth by a few peeps into my "memory basket." As other men have kept diaries all their lives, I have always kept a memory basket, in which, from earliest childhood, I have packed away all the touching little souvenirs of my everyday life. Each August 18th—in commemoration of the day I smoked my first marihuana cigarette—I run through this precious memory basket item by item, bedewing each with a nostalgic tear. Let me share a few of my keepsakes with you, my friends—in chronological order, of course.

First there is that dear baby tooth, with a small tag attached reading: "The first bicuspid that Little Willie lost. Extracted from Daddy's wrist on April 5, 1887." What a shining pearl it is, too—not a trace of a filling in it!

"—in commemoration of the day I smoked my first marihuana cigarette—"

(© 1939, Universal Pictures)

Next I find a fond note from my first-grade teacher to my mother, reporting my prodigious scholastic progress:

Dear Mrs. Fields:

Unless you can dissuade your son William from blowing his nose on the pen-wipers, I shall have to request you to keep him at home.

Sympathetically

Esther N. Pertwee

The next important memento affords a revealing glimpse into my adolescent character, which seems to have been of a serious, almost brooding, nature. It is a page ripped from the autograph book of the girl who sat next to me in Algebra-1. I remember her name was Rena, though I cannot recall for the nonce the square on her hypotenuse. This is what it says:

Name: W. C. Fields
Address: 1312 Grub Terrace
Favorite Flower: Coriopsis
Favorite Book: "113 Bird Calls—and How to Simulate Them"
What Color Do You Wear Most?—Size 14½
Favorite Hobby: Crocheting Antimacassars
If you were alone on a desert island with me, what would you
   do?— I would rub two sticks together to induce flame.

Here the fragment ends. But I am glad to say that the next keepsake is proof that my hobbyistic leanings, at least, soon become more virile. That keepsake—one of

my most precious treasures—is an exquisite pair of
loaded dice, bearing the date of my graduation from
high school.

Incidentally, it is of interest to note that I have remained true to the hobby of crap-shooting ever since,
and on this I rely for a great many votes. For nothing
will elect a President quicker than a hobby (unless it is
the ability to wear an Indian hat becomingly). Just for
instance, take the following Prexies:

Grover Cleveland . . . Fishing
Calvin Coolidge . . . Mechanical horseback riding
Franklin D. Roosevelt . . . Stamp collecting, in collab-
    oration with James A. Farley
Ulysses S. Grant . . . Well, of all the Presidents' hobbies,
    I think General Grant's came nearer to my ideas and
    ideals—excepting that I was never a great cigar
    smoker.

But let us drop the matter for the present and con-
tinue with the story of my early life. Upon being grad-
uated from high school I was at a loss to know what
profession to turn to. I knew little of law, and medicine
had always been distasteful to me. I might have made
a fine pianist except that a revolving stool always made
me dizzy. So, perforce, there was only one profession
left—juggling.

I proved a born genius in my chosen work, and between the years 1905 and 1908 I performed before

most of the crowned heads of Europe. Then came a tragic interlude of enforced retirement—during the spring of 1909 when my hand was caught in a pickle jar.

"Well, of all the Presidents' hobbies, I think General Grant's came nearer to my ideas and ideals—"

The Bank Dick (© 1940, Universal Pictures)

"So, perforce, there was only one profession left—juggling."

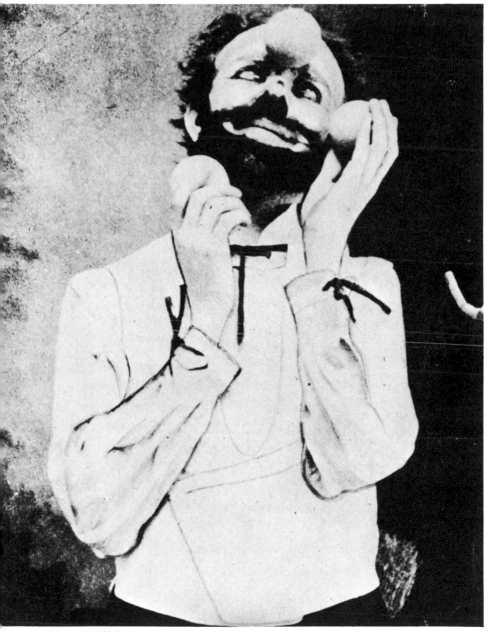

(Early 1900's)

Of course, from 1910 on, my meteoric march to the pinnacle of success has been immortalized in the songs and literature of our day, so it would seem needless to repeat the tale here.

Suffice it to say, because of the length and breadth of my experience, I have been showered with countless honorary degrees from our foremost universities. Many are the scholars who have sat at my feet. I particularly remember Nicholas Murray Butler and William Lyon Phelps, sitting cross-legged before the great open fireplace and staring up at me in awe. "Tell us more," they would beg. Fine fellows, Nick and Bill.

Naturally, in the last twenty or thirty years I have become the supreme authority on a good many matters that directly affect the everyday life of all people. Indeed, they are the very matters in which the chief executive of a great nation should of necessity be well-versed. Allow me to enumerate:

1. *Marriage:* Since approximately half the population of the United States is made up of the fairer sex, any President worthy of the name should be familiar with the intricacies of the matrimonial problem—unless he wants to change his residence from the White House to the *château de la chien* (doghouse).

2. *Income Tax:* The major responsibility of a President is to squeeze the last possible cent out of the taxpayer; thus he should be at least familiar with the intricacies of the ransom notes that the Internal Reve-

"A President must know how to keep himself fit—"

nue Department sends out each spring.

3. *Resolutions:* If the chief executive is not an expert in the art of making resolutions, how can he hope to break his campaign promises gracefully?

4. *Etiquette:* At a state dinner, should the Nazi ambassador be served *Châteaubriand à la Marseillaise?* Failure to understand this delicate question might well plunge our nation into war.

5. *Physical Fitness:* There is no room in the White House for a man who is afflicted with barber's itch, spots before the eyes, hangnails or housemaid's knee. A President must know how to keep himself fit—else

(Late 1930's)

who would throw out the first ball at the Washington Senators' opening game?

6. *The Care of Babies:* Shall didies be folded square or triangular? This is the burning question of the day,

"The Care of Babies: . . . the better the candidate understands the little darlings, the more competently he can decide the issue."

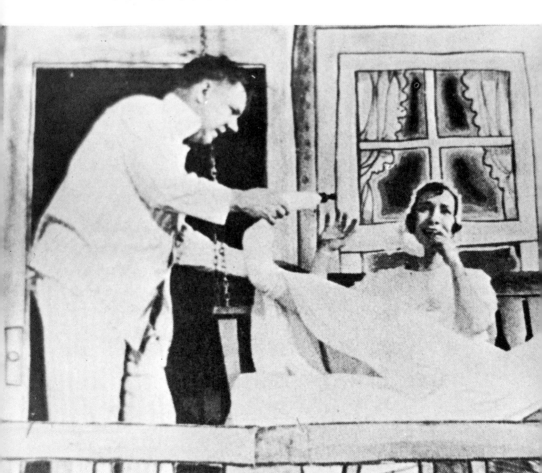

Ziegfeld Follies of 1921

and the better the candidate understands the little darlings, the more competently he can decide the issue.

7. *Business Success:* If he knows nothing else, a President should at least understand the secret of success in the business world. For, after all, what is the Presidency but a glorified business—or, at least, a fine racket?

Because of my broad understanding of these seven vital subjects, I commend myself to the great American public as the one and only logical choice for President in 1940. And in the succeeding chapters of this modest volume, I shall attempt to clarify my stand on every phase of each of the seven issues in question—as well as drop a few invaluable hints that will benefit each and every one of my readers.

And now, before we proceed further, let us all repair to the bar—the votes are on me.

Chapter 2

My Views on Marriage

> *"The leaders of our nation realize that in W. C. Fields they have a candidate who understands the fairer sex as well as the fiercer."*

Mrs. Wiggs of the Cabbage Patch (© 1934, Paramount Pictures)

Although married for a short time (then separated, though never legally divorced), Fields never had a very high regard for that institution. He felt marriage was a crutch for the weak and an infringement on man's independence.

Never one to let personal gripes slide by unnoticed, he took every opportunity to interject his personal denouncements on the subject into his comedy. His attitudes were summed up in a quote from Mississippi (Paramount, 1935), in which he nasaled: "A woman's like an elephant—I like to look at 'em, but I wouldn't want to own one!"

"One young lady—blond, about twenty-four years old, weighing in the neighborhood of 8 stone 6, picnic type..."

My Little Chickadee (© 1940, Universal Pictures)

TWENTY-ODD years ago, when I was the leading attraction of Hubert's Flea Circus, I used to saw a woman in half twice every evening, and thereby got a finer cross section of American femininity than most Fifth Avenue psychiatrists.

This knowledge will stand me in good stead when I take over at Washington. For it is one thing to have to explain to a man why a billion-dollar measure has been vetoed; but it is much more difficult to explain to a woman why the cap of the toothpaste tube has not been put back on.

The leaders of our nation realize that in W. C. Fields they have a candidate who understands the fairer sex as well as the fiercer. In fact, just a year ago last Michaelmas, Dorothy Dix said to me: "William [that is what the "W" stands for], if every man in the nation understood marriage as you do, America would be a different country today." I can't recall for the nonce what country she said America would be, but in any event, it was a compliment I shall treasure through the years.

Every day in the week harassed young men and women seek my sage counsel concerning their marital problems. "Should I reveal my past?" they ask. One young lady—blond, about twenty-four years old, weighing in the neighborhood of 8 stone 6, picnic type (I prefer to withhold her name)—fell upon my shoulder (the left one) and sobbed like a swaddling babe. "Shall I tell him? Shall I tell him? Shall I tell him?" (referring to her husband, of course) she cried over and over again. A stimulant was necessary. In fact, I ordered two and had one myself. "Do you know a Mexican lawyer?" she intoned coyly prior to my assisting her through the side entrance into a taxi.

Before I could answer, the taxi was off like a bat out of the habitat of Old Ned. "Never mind a lawyer. Tell your husband nothing about it. He may never find it out. Never smarten up a chump!" I shouted repeatedly, running down Broadway after the taxi.

My patience with these pitiable human beings is infinite. Marriage is a double, vast adventure, the depths of which few have plumbed. And because of my wide experience in plumbing (both indoor and out) I feel it my bounden duty to enlighten the many thousands of my weaker brothers and sisters—poor devils—who are groping in the dark.

Right at the outset, friends (I always think of my

readers as friends and would like to ask you all to a libation if I thought a quart would go around), I wish to state unbiasedly and without reservations that most marriage problems of today stem from the fact that we pamper our gentle sex too much. The nation needs to return to the colonial trend of life, when a wife was judged by the amount of wood she could split or buckets of coal she could carry up from the cellar. But probably that is asking too much of human nature. The old order changeth, *o tempora, o mores!* The young men of today prefer to consider their fair ones as frail flowers and parade their own manly strength before them. (Personally, I am of the old school.)

This is a mistake! *Never try to impress a woman!* Because if you do she'll expect you to keep up to the standard for the rest of your life. And the pace, my friends, is devastating.

I tried to impress a woman once. Abigail Twirlbaffing was her name and she lived next door to us. Played left field for the Guthrie Centre Hay & Grain Co. Dodgers, batting 835. Abigail bestowed upon me the befitting appellation of "Blondie," and I always addressed her as "My Plum." In those days I could blow a bugle harder than an Eagle Scout. I once blew a bugle so hard that after one blast of Reveille it looked like a trombone. Ultimately an opportunity afforded itself and I got a chance to play cornet in the town band. The cornetist had been run down by a pie wagon—the unfortunate poor dear! I practiced day and night and sometimes in the afternoon. One evening after the ball game, little Abigail came over to listen. She was all intent. I wanted to impress her. I held my breath for a few moments—then I ripped off "The Whistler and His Dog." I gave it my all. "You wonderful man!" she gasped and fainted. She had a look in her eyes like that of a wild horse. My heart bled for her. My intuition tells me how a woman suffers when she is in love with a great artist.

"I could play that backwards," I calmly admitted and, to *impress* her, of course, I suited the action to the words, with the music upside down and the notes facing the audience, which had gathered from a near-by bowling alley. Then I played on one foot. Pandemonium broke loose. Well, friends, Abigail's eyes got wilder. I was led on. "And now," I boasted in stentorian tones, "I shall play it forwards and backwards at the same time." Then with my index and middle fingers I played "The Whistler and His Dog" forwards, and with my fourth and little finger, or pinkie, I played it backwards. Believe me, friends, it was a memorable performance. Every note, every nuance rang forth *furioso con fortissimo*—until suddenly the two parts met up in the middle with a terrific backfire that knocked two of my front teeth out!

Abigail immediately threw me over. She said she could never marry a man who wore bridgework.

That is why I say, *never try to impress a woman.*

If there were only one other piece of advice I could

give a young man it would be this: marry a woman who cannot read.

I have found in my extensive research on modern marriage that the morning newspaper is the cause of

"'You wonderful man!' she gasped and fainted."

You Can't Cheat an Honest Man (© 1939, Paramount Pictures)

13.4% (as of March 14, 1940) of all marital disasters.
Of the women who can read in America, nine out of ten
have not an iota of respect for a newspaper. After they

*"Of the women who can read in America, nine out of
ten have not an iota of respect for a newspaper."*

Man on the Flying Trapeze (© 1935, Paramount Pictures)

get through with one in the morning it looks as though it had been used to pack crockery. Worse than that, the running order of the pages has been completely altered.

I know of at least one case where this has led to tragic results. One of the most promising young men I ever knew, Clarence Fritt, married a young lady who, when she got her hands on a daily, became a veritable fiend. One morning the young lad met his boss in the elevator. "How did Roosevelt's last message to Congress get across?" asked the boss. "He had the whole House of Representatives behind him," answered the young man, "until the Yankees squeezed through two runs in the eleventh inning; then General Motors dropped half a point and it looks like partly cloudy with occasional showers tomorrow."

Needless to relate, the poor boy got the old heave-o next payday.

If there is another feminine failing that rivals newspaper vivisection for disastrous consequences, it is the habit of *putting things away*. Beware, brother, of the super-tidy wife. Some years ago a nephew of mine, whom I loved as dearly as one *can* love a nephew, married a lovely fledgling whose only fault was putting things away. The very first month she put away his gray sweater with the grease spot on the sleeve (which is synonymous with putting moths on relief). She soon became bolder and put away his old straw hat, his cracked mandolin, his prized collection of beer mats, and even the autographed barrel stave that was used on him at his fraternity initiation. Then the fever was upon her. She started putting away books, pictures, old magazines, tobacco tins and steins. Ultimately, one warm afternoon when my nephew was dozing on the sofa, she cracked up entirely and put *him* away!

That was in the spring of the year Bryan quit the Cabinet and we haven't found hide nor hair of the poor devil since. Some say he is living in Jersey City, which only complicates things.

Now, every fair-minded reader will concede that this was unreasonable on the part of my nephew's wife, even though he had never contributed a farthing to her support. (Money isn't everything.) Unreasonableness on the part of American wives is perhaps the greatest single cause of marital tragedy today. The wife who carps at her husband's cleaning his boots on the bedroom curtain is merely digging her own matrimonial grave. A man must look tidy, if for business reasons only.

I know of a couple who had lived happily together sixteen years until the wife's unreasonableness finally shattered both their lives. One day, after a grueling eighteen holes on the golf links (missing nearly every putt after wonderful woods and irons) and an equally hard evening in the locker room, the husband came home and literally toppled into bed. And when he tried to soothe his aching feet on his wife's back, *she actually rose and went into the guest room to sleep.* Well! I leave it to you.

"A man must look tidy, if for business reasons only."

"One day, after a grueling eighteen holes on the golf links . . . and an equally hard evening in the locker room . . ."

(Mid-1930's. University of Texas)

Naturally, it was such a wound to his feelings that their relationship was wrecked. The wife later denied that she had been unreasonable on the grounds that the poor fellow had been too fatigued to remove his spiked shoes, but I have always regarded it as a flimsy excuse.

So, my gentle feminine readers, next time your husband stamps out a cigarette on the living room rug, take stock of *yourself* before you pout at him. Possibly the fault lies at your own door.

For instance, you may be among the 83% of American wives who have an unbridled passion for microscopic ash trays. There is nothing so bewildering to husbands as to have nothing large enough to cram an ash into. Recently I was a guest at the home of a demure young bride of scarce a month. I chanced to flick my ashes on the rug.

"Listen, you red-nosed wart hog," she jollied me. "Where were you brought up, in a horse stall?" (There is a possibility she wasn't only twitting.)

"There, there, my little song sparrow," I soothed her. "I'm merely giving you an object lesson, and if you are wise, you will heed it. You are addicted to minute ash trays. If you do not overcome the failing, it will some day break up your home. I once had an experience that proved nearly fatal. A niece of mine back in Oglethorpe, Georgia, was a bride of three months when she went to an afternoon bridge party and won a pair of infinitesimal ivory ash trays. She sent them to me—her loving uncle. One evening, suffering from a severe headache,

I swallowed them with a glass of water. I thought they were aspirin tablets."

But aside from these minor incidents of marital difficulty, I must return to my original point—that the woman of today is too pampered. I have a letter before me at this very moment—wait a second—ah, here it is —from a housewife who says that her husband is away from home twenty-three hours out of the day, only bothering to come home to change his shirt. She feels that not only is she losing his devotion but that time hangs heavy on her hands.

My only answer is that probably the fault lies with her. I almost insist on this—that if she would keep busier, her husband would become more devoted, and she would never again have to worry about holding his love. And this advice applies to any wife anywhere.

There you have it. Read my book, "Fields' Formula for Fretting Females." It includes the following schedule, which I have drawn up at the request of countless home-economics bureaus:

THE FIELDS FORMULA FOR
FRETTING FEMALES

7:00–8:00: Arise quietly, shake down furnace, stoke it, prepare breakfast—eggs exactly four minutes, two lumps in the Java!

8:00–8:10: Awake husband *gently*, singing *sotto voce*. My preferences would be "Narcissus" or "Silent Night."

9:00–10:00: Drive husband to station, do marketing for dinner, and be sure not to order anything husband might decide to have for lunch.

10:00–12:00: Mow lawn, wash clothes, iron husband's shirts, press his suits, paint screens, weed garden, swat flies.

12:00–2:00: Clean cellar, wash windows, tidy house, beat rugs.

2:00–2:15: Eat simple lunch.

2:15–5:30: Spade garden, darn socks, wash Rover, put up jelly, polish car, burn rubbish, wash woodwork, paint garage, clean side walls of tires.

5:30–7:00: Drive to station for husband, shake cocktails, cook dinner, serve dinner, wash dishes.

7:00–12:00: Keep busy—keep smiling—for, as every man knows, the husband is tired.

I think, my friends, that *that* just about covers the subject of marriage.

Chapter **3**

*How to Beat the Federal
Income Tax—and What to
See and Do at Alcatraz*

(Early 1900's)

Fields' income tax practices were very amusing. He regularly made huge deductions for blatantly ridiculous items; one year he claimed $25,000 for milk, as an entertainment expense for newsmen. One especially padded year he received a rebate on a new and similarly preposterous subterfuge. Far from being pleased, Fields was furious at having missed employing this ruse in the past. His lawyer was barely able to dissuade the Great Man from trying to sue the government for past losses on this account by reminding him of the lengthy jail term possible should anyone choose to examine his records. The indignant Fields spent the next few weeks denouncing the unorthodox practices of "Uncle Whiskers."

". . . the government fixes it so that you have a choice of (1) starving to death by having an income so low that you do not have to pay a tax; or (2) having an income high enough to pay a tax—and then starving to death after you've paid it."

> *"I number at least one such person among my acquaintances (I say "number" because that is what he is now —at Alcatraz, pronounced Al-cat-razz)."*

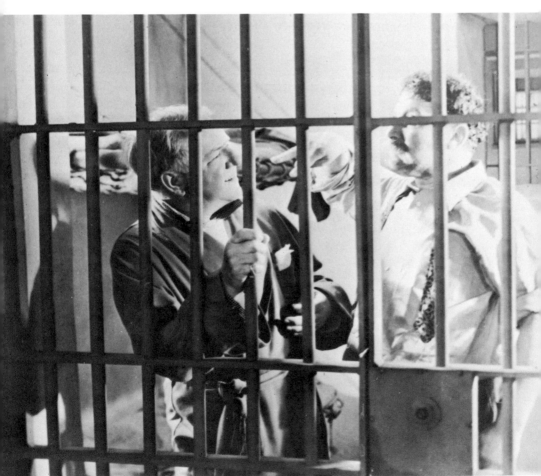

Trapeze (© 1935, Paramount Pictures)

MARCH 15 is always a day of rare rejoicing and unbridled revelry throughout the nation. For that is the day when all the citizens of our fair land may practice their inalienable rights of sending a fat slice of their yearly increments to Washington; in return, our Congressmen will forward packages of radish seed or intimate candid-camera shots of themselves weeding their farms or kissing their grandchildren. Most Congressmen are very human, if nothing else.

Among my myriads of gentle readers, there are doubtless a goodly number whose appreciation of March 15 is marred only by the intricacies of wrestling with an income-tax blank. Forsooth, there are some citizens who feel so cowed by this imposing document that they ignore it altogether. I number at least one such person among my acquaintances (I say "number" because that is what he is now—at Alcatraz, pronounced Al-cat-razz).

And yet, filling out an income-tax blank is as easy as rolling off a logarithm; just to prove it, my friends, I will lead you step by step through the process. And do not for a moment fear that I shan't be meticulously correct in every statement. Correctness runs in the Fields family. Even today I can remember how often Daddy used to declare: "I'd rather be correct than be President." As a matter of fact, that is probably the reason he skipped the White House and ended up in the House of Correction.

But to get down to business: In order to pay an income tax you must first have an income, and that income must be in excess of $1,000. In other words, the government fixes it so that you have a choice of (1) starving to death by having an income so low that you do not have to pay a tax; or (2) having an income high enough to pay a tax—and then starving to death after you've paid it.

This is a plan that is not only fundamentally false, but also shamefully misleading. Take, for instance, the case of a friend of mine, Mr. O'Hare, who took out his citizenship papers many years ago and worked like a Trojan, day in and day out, as a tonsorial artist. After thirty-five years of standing behind a barber's chair, discussing the affairs of the day, touching up every subject from Ty Cobb's unethical antics on the field to the tax the Governor should put on gum drops—all the while trying to make himself heard above the customers' snores—he still could not make enough to lift himself into the income-tax class.

But he was a man of ambition, so he finally developed a sure-fire business idea. He opened a new barber shop and engaged deaf-and-dumb barbers who couldn't even write. Thereby the customers were permitted to think whilst being tonsorialized, and to pick their own winners. The bootblack was deaf and dumb, too.

The news of his unique new venture spread like wildflowers. Mr. O'Hare opened tonsorial emporiums in every large city and hamlet from the rock-bound coast of Maine to the snow-capped mountains of California. As an added attraction he engaged deaf-and-dumb manicurists with dark hair.

Money poured in so thick and fast that his estranged wife, on advice of her relatives and counsel, decided it was the better part of value to sue him immediately for alimony and community property. She sued on March 2, 1937.

Alas! There was nothing to sue for. For, while a short time ago Mr. O'Hare was only a poor barber and consequently had no business paying an income tax, today he was paying an income tax and consequently had no business.

However, I am not the type to dictate, and if any of my readers want to be as foolish as Mr. O'Hare, and go and make $1,000 and more, so be it. I will try to guide them even in their folly.

So follow me closely while I delve into detail. In the first place, here are the principal things needed in filling out an income tax: one dozen tax blanks, six pencils, one slide rule, one Chinese abacus, three reams of inexpensive copy paper, an ice pack and various medicinal stimulants.

The first thing to do is print your name plainly on the proper line. If it is a joint return, we are instructed to print the given names of both husband and wife. But since some of the names that husband and wife give each other are hardly suited to print, we must proceed cautiously.

After you have filled in this information, the next matter you'll think of is what you can deduct and what you can't deduct, always keeping in mind the possibility that a tall man with a dark mustache and a blue serge suit and a gold star might come to the house with a piece of paper. Most of us know already that torn postage stamps are not deductible items; nor is the cost of telegrams to Senators asking that they reduce the income-tax rate; or the box of cigars you forgot to give the postman last Christmas.

But there are other questions of deduction that the general public is not so well informed upon. For instance, most of us are under the impression that Bad Debts can be deducted. I can assure each and every one of my ardent readers that this is not the case at all. Last year I tried to deduct a dentist bill of $143.00, which was one of my very worst debts, but it was disallowed. This hurt me worse than the dentist.

At any rate, here is my best advice on the matter of

deductions: just count off on your fingers all the items that you suspect might be deductible—and then forget them, because they aren't.

Now that that issue is settled, the rest of the income-tax problem falls into two divisions: whether you can add and subtract straight to arrive at your tax total; and whether you can pay the total once you arrive at it.

The first is a mere question of arithmetic, and will be dealt with further on in this pronunciamento. The second—how to scrape up the dough—is of extreme im-

"—how to scrape up the dough—is of extreme importance, and I should like to clear the matter up here and now."

My Little Chickadee (© 1940, Universal Pictures)

portance, and I should like to clear the matter up here and now.

With this in mind, let me say that I am a strong advocate of budgeting throughout the year so that in March the difficulty of paying one's income tax will be no difficulty at all. I recommend it to all my readers because I have seen budgeting work such wonders in the past. Of course an improperly arranged budget is apt to be more of a hindrance than a help. For instance, less than a month ago a young man came to me with tears in his eyes. He had run into the knottiest sort of a budgetary problem, and he begged me for expert advice. Here is how he had arranged his weekly budgeting schedule:

1.	Income tax	$ 0.26
2.	Carfare	0.60
3.	Room rent	4.50
4.	Food	3.83
5.	Clothing	1.27
6.	Medicinal spirits	19.54
		$30.00

Of course my practical mind grasped the basic trouble immediately. I merely advised him to shave down on the first five items and put the savings into bicarbonate of soda.

As a matter of fact, this lad's mistakes reminded me

not a little of our own government's budgetary errors. Only too often do they pile up headaches without providing for relief. This will all be changed when I become chief executive of our fair land. To provide funds for a free public headache-powder service, I shall charge Pullman rates to all Congressmen caught sleeping in session.

But to give all you dear, *dear* folks a graphic example of the miracles a well-balanced budget can achieve, I am going to set down, right before your eyes, a word-for-word first-of-March conversation in the household of the Homer N. Cluffs, a typical American family consisting of one husband, one wife, one three-year-old son and a canary that has just started to molt. The Cluffs were kind enough to allow the W. C. Fields Budgetary Research Foundation to install a dictograph in their cozy little living room. I quote from the record:

Homer: Now, my phlox, my flower, let us look over the budget envelopes and straighten out the month's expenses. Income tax is due in two weeks, you know.

Lucretia: Yes, pet, here are all fourteen envelopes.

Homer: Fine! Now, Income Tax amounts to thirty-seven dollars.

Lucretia: Something is wrong! There's only eleven dollars in Income Tax!

Homer: What? There *must* be more. All I took was sixteen dollars for those new golf clubs.

Lucretia: Oh, dear! I can't think where it went to—unless I took the money for my last permanent out of this envelope.

"*. . . the household of Homer N. Cliffs, a typical American family . . .*"

Homer: Well, for Pete's sake, why didn't you take it out of Incidentals in the first place?

Lucretia: Now, you *know* we paid the insurance premium out of Incidentals.

Homer (weakly): Is there an aspirin or an analine-dye tablet in the house?

Lucretia: I'm sorry, dear, we're all out of them.

Homer: Never mind, let's make up Income Tax out of Savings. We'll double Savings next month.

Lucretia: For pity's sake! There's only six dollars in Savings.

Homer: Now, look! The only money I took out of that envelope was eight dollars for the plumber.

Lucretia: I—I guess I must have taken out a teentsy bit for the first installment on my mink coat.

Homer: Teentsy bit! Mink coat! Godfrey Daniel! What do you think the Clothing envelope's for?

"Mink coat! Godfrey Daniel!"

Lucretia: Now, Homer, you *must* remember that we used Clothing to pay off the Smiths that night we played for a quarter of a cent a point and you went down four tricks doubled and vulnerable.

Homer (hoarsely): I'm going down to the drugstore for some aspirin. Give me a dime out of Medical Attention.

Lucretia: Medical Attention's already gone for Amy's wedding present. But there's a couple of ginger-ale bottles under the sink —take those.

Well, my friends, I think this sprightly little interlude should prove to even the most skeptical that budgeting *can* help you to pay your income tax painlessly. *But*—and this is a big but—the mere fact that you *can* pay your income tax will avail you little unless you are able to sum up what your tax should be. Thusly, I will now plunge into the arithmetical phase of the income-tax problem, as I promised I would.

Many of our most successful citizens have forgotten even the rudiments of arithmetic they learned in school.

Therefore, for the benefit of any of my readers and those who repeat this incident to their friends and any who may be weak in their ciphers, I will run through an exercise in simple addition. To add a realistic touch, I will use as a model the income tax I myself filed last March.

Here is the sum—or something:

Salaries, compensations $7,180
Dividends 2,370

Interest on bank deposits, etc.   1,260
Interest on corporation bonds   3,140
Income from fiduciaries ....   ?
(This last is a knotty technical phrase con-
cerning which you have to see your attor-
ney.)

The usual procedure is, first, to add up the rows of
figures farthest to the right. Now, it is plain to even the
layman's eye that the four zeros are equal to nothing
at all, so we may ignore that row altogether. However,
the figures in the second row from the right add up to
25, and that brings us to a very tricky piece of business.
The first thing to do, under these conditions, is to write
down the 5 neatly, with calm determination, thus:

5

The 2 in the 25 must be disposed of by a process
called "carrying," but to understand that, you must
know solid geometry; so just take my word for it that
you should add it in with the third row of figures. This
row, with the 2 included, adds to 9—a dismal number
indeed! For the last twenty years I have made it a strict
policy to avoid the number 9. It probably all stems
back to the summer of 1920, when I played third base
for the Germanic-Amerikanisch Brewing Company
Nine. Whenever the team traveled out of town for a
game, it was a standing rule that the last player into the
hotel room at night had to sleep on the floor.

Of course, I realize that my aversion to the figure 9

is not shared by the nation as a whole, but I'm sure that few would begrudge me the whim of changing it to 8 in this case. So our total so far stands at:

85

The column farthest to the left adds up to 13—and I can get a C. P. A. to vouch for it. However, everyone knows that 13 is fast becoming obsolete these days. As a matter of fact, apartment buildings and office blocks don't even have thirteenth floors any more. But a Fields is nothing if not magnanimous, so let's throw in the 3, at least. Thus our final total turns out to be:

$385

Of course, I realize that it is not easy for my dear pupils to understand, at first glance, all the mammoth complications by which I arrived at this interesting figure. However, the boys down at the Internal Revenue office have had long experience with my remarkable mathematical prowess, and they will doubtless follow me in short order.

It might be apropos to mention here that Federal finances closely resemble personal income taxes, and are added up much the same as I have just demonstrated. The only difference is that in the case of Federal figures, a great many zeroes are added to the end of each item. I do not hesitate to proclaim myself one of the craftiest adders in the country (and if a President can do nothing else, he *must* be able to add and add). I also have an uncanny knack of describing circles, so I am sure I could outzero any other candidate

"*However, the boys down at the Internal Revenue office have had long experience with my remarkable
mathematical prowess, and they will doubtless follow
me in short order.*"

My Little Chickadee (© 1940, Universal Pictures)

—with the possible exception of F. D. R. himself.

Well, we must be getting on to multiplication—an extremely important subject. In fact, the government gives prizes of $400 exemptions for multiplication. . . . But pardon me for a moment—there goes the doorbell. My little son Warner looking out the window informs me: "That man is here again."

Ah, it's the Internal Revenue inspector. "How do you do, Inspector. . . . You say they're asking for me down at the Collector of Internal Revenue's office? Well, I suppose I can spare an hour or so, if they're really in a bad tangle. . . . What's that? You say 'come quietly'? Why, Inspector, you cut me to the core! (Oh, Mrs. Fields, don't wait up for me tonight, dear. I may not be home for a year or two.)"

"You say they're asking for me down at the Collector of Internal Revenue's office?"

The Bank Dick (© 1940, Universal Pictures)

Chapter 4

"Fields, a Man
of Firm Resolve"

Ziegfeld Follies of 1919 (University of Texas)

When Whitey (a childhood nickname) made up his mind on a subject, he was immovable. This was especially so concerning his comedy. He had been in show business most of his life and quite reasonably felt he knew more about humor and reaching an audience than did all of his writers and directors combined. Often when disputes arose, he would retire to his dressing room and bring an entire production to a costly halt. Once, after a particularly heated dispute, he returned home and shut himself off from the numerous emissaries sent by the studio. After a few days, Samuel Goldwyn (then president of M.G.M.) himself arrived. The stunned butler, hesitant about snubbing one of the most powerful men in Hollywood, went to Fields for specific instructions. "Give him an evasive answer," replied the inscrutable Fields. "Be evasive. Tell him to go — himself!"

"A hair off'n the dog that bit me."

Running Wild (© 1927, Paramount Pictures)

CAMPAIGN resolutions are nothing more than overgrown New Year's resolutions: they are thrown together hastily at the last minute, with never a thought as to how they may be gracefully broken.

Now, I am a candidate with years of experience in the making and breaking of New Year's resolutions, and what I can accomplish with those, I can certainly accomplish with campaign resolutions.

From my long months of study on the question of New Year's resolutions I have come to many important conclusions. In the first place, as I mentioned above, too many of us are inclined to put off New Year's resolutions until 11 A.M. New Year's morning, when we wake up in white tie and tails, and mumble "a hair off'n the dog that bit me." This is a sad mistake. Remorse runs rampant at such a time, and we are liable to consign ourselves to all sorts of extravagant penances, such as hying ourselves to monasteries in Tibet or Afghanistan, or spending our remaining days in Brooklyn to atone for numerous things.

I myself was the victim of the 11 A.M. Menace several years ago. The evening preceding January first, I was invited to a party by a couple who intended to get married (which they did, but not to each other). I awoke New Year's Day to find a full-grown goat in bed beside me; worse than that, my head felt as though a manhole cover were resting on it. Imagine my surprise and chagrin when I reached up and found that there *was* a manhole cover resting on my head! You could have knocked me down with a cricket racquet, or club (or whatever they use) or a slapstick bass fiddle or— but why quibble? Right then and there I swore that I would never again poison my system with a maraschino cherry. Of course, it wasn't two weeks before I slipped. Hoodwinked, yes. I thought it was a seedless grape. I washed it down with some snake-bite remedy that Grandpa always kept in a downstairs closet.

That is why, my friends, I am making this desperate plea that the citizens of our nation avoid making reckless resolutions. This plea is particuraly directed to the Little Women of America, bless their dear souls. I love every one of them (the California Anti-Heartbalm Law will be in effect by the time this is printed). According to figures—those who follow the game closely will know what I mean—over 80% of reckless resolutions made by American husbands occur at a moment when the wife is standing over the bed with a putter in her hand, giving advice and making certain demands.

Of course, I fully sympathize with the good intentions of the fair sex in this matter. But too often they

"I awoke New Year's Day to find a full-grown goat in bed beside me."

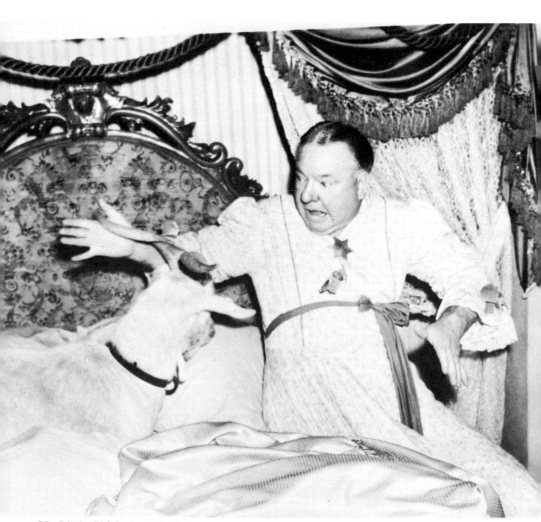

My Little Chickadee (© 1940, Universal Pictures)

do not realize what hardships these—shall we say "forced"—resolutions are going to mean to their husbands, the stronger or more formidable sex, if I may coin a phrase.

For instance, one day just last October (it may have been November; however, it was prior to the first flurry) I was hurrying to a florist friend for a bunch of goldenrod to send my mother-in-law (the poor dear was suffering with a stubborn case of hay fever). As I strolled along at a spry clip, my shoelace chanced to come undone. I stopped in at the neighborhood taproom to tie it. Once in the taproom my attention was drawn to a medium-sized, middle-aged chap who was stumbling about with his eyes tightly closed. His yelps of pain when he barked his shins on chairs and tables distressed me sorely.

"Can't that poor fellow open his eyes?" I asked the proprietor.

"Certainly he could—if he wanted to," answered that worthy, gruffly. "But last New Year's he promised his wife that he'd never look at a drop of whiskey again as long as he lived, and Dave's the kind of a chap who keeps his word!"

Now, Dave was doubtless a man of strong character whose rigid childhood training had inculcated in him a respect for New Year's resolutions that he never out-

"...a bunch of goldenrod to send to my mother-in-law (the poor dear was suffering with a stubborn case of hay fever)."

(Early 1940's)

grew. It is interesting to note that I myself had just such training in my youth. I remember a beautiful and inspiring little poem my mother used to recite to us children each New Year's Eve before we went to bed. It went thus:

> Let's make a resolution true,
>   And firm and good and healthful, too,
> But we must promise when we make it,
>   That we shall never, never—

(I can't remember the last two words but the whole poem was beautifully written in Spencerian hand.)

All through my grammar-school years these lovely lines had a great influence on me, and I can remember that once I even made a resolution that I would no longer spend my Sunday-school-offering nickel at the candy store. I kept this up for seven months, but finally my pocket became so full of nickels that I could not play Run Sheep Run with the other boys. The whole incident rather knocked my faith in resolutions into a cocked hat (though I admit I seldom wore one—never found a hat store that kept them in stock. They always had to send to Philadelphia for them and could never guarantee delivery). And for the next few years I made only a few infinitesimal resolutions, just so I'd have something to give up in Lent.

But soon even these began to irk me—so I finally devised a perfect plan for making resolutions, one which

"The whole incident rather knocked my faith in resolutions into a cocked hat."

(© 1940, Universal Pictures)

has stood me in good stead ever since.

In any event, if my gentle readers wish to take advantage of this simple plan, full directions are given herewith:

Early in November the prospective resolutioner should set aside an evening, settle himself in an easy chair before a fire of eucalyptus logs and, whilst sipping a cup of Iron Mountain Elixir and Exhilarator, write down carefully all the luxuries of life he can forego without endangering his peace of mind or health. For instance, tripe, pedicures, snuff, hair singes, cello lessons, croquet, flinch, etc. When he has finally decided on which he wishes to give up, he should telephone his solicitor and direct him to draw up a statement that will leave a few loopholes in case the strain grows too great on his nerves or impairs his health during the fatal ensuing twelve months.

The following is a contract I had drawn up in 1931, two months after the head of a certain studio kicked me below the spine and yelled at the top of his voice, "Git!" I have always considered this document a meticulous model of jurisprudence and foresight:

"I, W. C. Fields, being of sound mind and body, agree that during the year of 1932 I will cease and desist from eating spun sugar except under the following circumstances: (1) If said spun sugar is forced upon me by a person or persons unknown, professional bartenders included. (2) If abovementioned spun sugar is disguised beyond reasonable recognition. (3) If spun sugar in question is the only means of sustenance available due to special and extraordinary circumstances, etc., ad libitum, I to be the judge."

This resolution I never had the slightest trouble with, and that is because I left myself *beaucoup*—meaning plenty (we are not all up on foreign languages)—of legal leeway.

I will take full advantage of such technicalities in making and breaking all my campaign resolutions. For instance, just now I am framing a very important resolution, namely, that I will lower the income tax and decrease government running expenses (assuming, of course, that there will be any such thing as income when I become President, and that the government will be running). Now, it is obvious that I could not lower the income tax without *increasing* government running expenses, because printing up revised income-tax forms would cost a fortune. Therefore, when I eventually break this resolution, it will be looked upon by the American public as a patriotic action.

The truth is—and this is the most daring statement I have ever made except where and when only circumstances altered my opinion for reasons best known to myself—*the whole custom of New Year's resolutions —as well as Presidential resolutions—is based on an insidious fault of logic!*

There, now, you have it—the whole unvarnished. And the amazing thing about it is that the fault is an extremely simple one, but for thousands of years—

may I add, many thousands of years?—mankind has entirely overlooked it. It has remained for one heroic individual of peerless ingenuity to put his mind to the problem and uncover the seemingly intangible solution. I speak modestly of W. C. Fields. I wish you could all see my face as I blushingly pen these lines.

I quote from my own work titled. "Inquiry into Self-Imposed Tortures" (the Malay States bought practically the whole edition): "Ninety-three per cent of New Year's resolutions fail because they are based on frustration. Tell a person he must no longer eat pomegranates, and he'll be a nervous wreck until he does eat them. Pomegranates *au rum,* à la Papa."

A good illustration of this was the case of a friend of mine whom we shall call A. His name began with M, but we'll still call him A, just to keep it scientific. A was in the habit of walking to work, and his path took him through the municipal zoo. He had walked through the zoo many thousand times and felt *au fait* (okey-dokey) on all occasions—until the fatal day when he saw a freshly-painted sign on the bars of the lions' cage: HANDS OFF! He began to fret, to feel jumpy and ill-natured. He stood it for three months, and then one Thursday morning, shortly after St. Swithin's Day, he stalked straight up to the HANDS OFF! sign and grabbed the bars of the cage firmly. Immediately his frustration disappeared completely—and two seconds later, to the tune of angry snorts and roars, so did his hands. The HANDS OFF! sign had been correct. That's the price that

"I wish you could all see my face as I blushingly pen these lines."

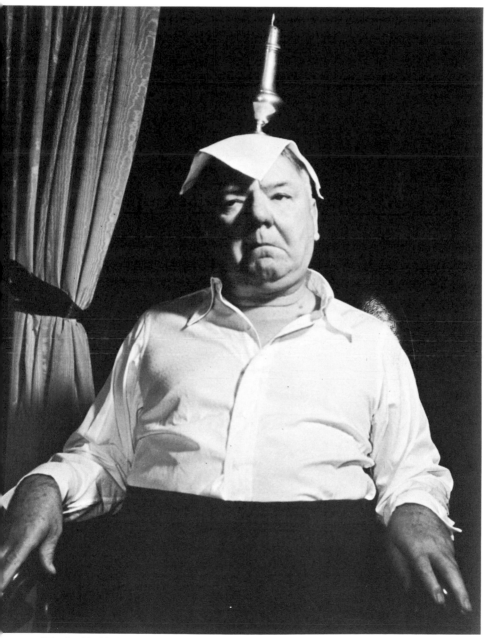

(Early 1940's. Photograph by Will Connell)

one man paid to get rid of his frustration—and he says it was worth it. "Would you like to play cards?" a friend one day a little later chided him. "Yes, deal me a couple of hands," was his curt rejoinder.

Frustration—that is the great trouble with America today. And if the nation would only grit its teeth and say, "I'm going to follow the Fields Plan next New Year's!" everything would iron itself out beautifully.

For the Fields Plan is so infinitely simple! It is based on one all-important, fundamental principle: instead of prohibiting a person from doing what he'd like to do, *force* him to do what he'd like to do. And it's all done with New Year's resolutions.

The Fields Plan is so pleasant that even I, myself, follow it. Here are the resolutions I drew up for my own personal use during 1940, but which I'll rent or sell outright to any of my readers who wish to adopt them. I think you'll find them frust rate. (I have inserted "frust rate" to add a bit of levity to a serious subject.)

FIELDS PLAN, FORMULA 31-B

Sundays: I resolve to go the reading room of the public library, hold the QUIET! sign over my head and sing "Asleep in the Deep."

Mondays: I resolve to enter every door I see marked PRIVATE— NO ADMITTANCE, and shout "BOO!" (Did I scare you?)

Tuesdays: I resolve to test all newly-laid concrete sidewalks by pressing my foot into them. (Crown Prince Gustave of somewhere or other wears the same size shoe as I do, which has nothing to do with it but I thought it worth mentioning.)

Wednesdays: I resolve to spend my lunch hour leaning against signs reading POSITIVELY NO LOITERING. (I may omit this. The weather will have oodles to do with it.)

Thursdays: I resolve to throw a brick through any plate-glass window that I feel is an unjust temptation. (I once did this where a gentleman was demonstrating a muscle-building exercise. Was he in perfect condition!)

Fridays: I resolve to apply the finger test to all objects marked WET PAINT.

Saturdays: I resolve to do the most intriguing thing of all: to pull the emergency cord on the 2:15 local! This is one way to make friends and influence commuters.

And so, my dear, gentle friends, I wish to say that to any who decide to follow this program, I can guarantee a truly Happy New Year. For, under the Fields Plan, you can swear off—swear on—or just swear.

And you needn't wait till January first to start your New Year. Any day will do. My own will began on November fifth, and I invite you all to come down to Washington on November sixth and break resolutions with me.

". . . and I invite you all to come down to Washington on November sixth and break resolutions with me."

The Old Fashioned Way (© 1934, Paramount Pictures)

Chapter 5

My Rules of Etiquette

Poppy (theater version, 1924)

Fields often used manners and etiquette to indicate his disapproval of those social amenities and impositions he found most offensive. He habitually wore an obnoxious clip on moustache to formal occasions (with tux or tails), if for no other reason than to let people know he was bending, but not beat! W. C. also found an ingeniously subtle method to signify his disapproval of the frequent visits made by his short termed mother-in-law. When she came for dinner, he would protest her presence most disconcertingly by sitting through the evening repast with a bottle of beer precariously perched atop his head, never making the vaguest reference to what his stupefied in-law must have assumed was a regular occurrence.

"As everyone knows, I have been a scholar of proper procedure . . ."

"Why, friends, there wasn't a lady over sixty in the whole village that I didn't raise my hat to—regularly."

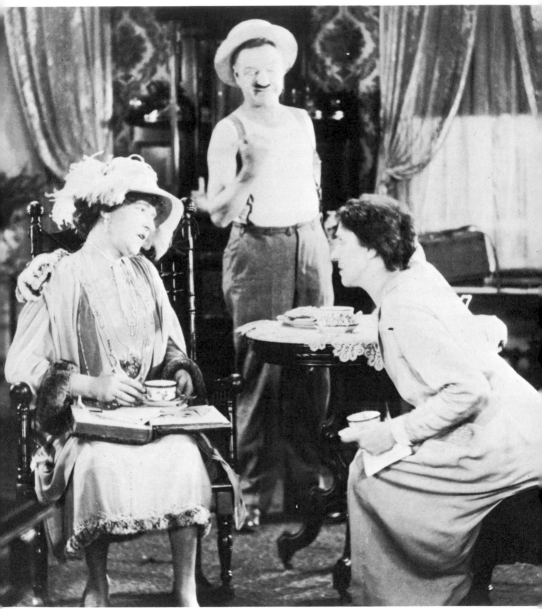

So's Your Old Man (Famous Players-Lasky Corp., 1926)

WHAT would you do if you were President, and, on the first day of May, the Russian Ambassador presented you with a beautiful cake which emitted a curious ticking noise? Would you plunge it into a pail of water—thus insulting Soviet *cuisine* in general? Or would you calmly take a knife and cut it, offering the first slice to the Ambassador with the remark, "I fondly trust I am giving you the works!"?

Ticklish little problems like this arise every day at the White House, and that is why it is imperative to have a man like me on the spot to pass them off gracefully. Because, as everyone knows, I have been a scholar of proper procedure ever since I was in short pants.

"Cavalier Will" they used to call me in my old home town. Why, friends, there wasn't a lady over sixty in the whole village that I didn't raise my hat to—regularly. And through all the years since, gentlemanliness has been my watchword.

Being of a modest nature, I have never publicly set myself up as a social arbiter. But, at last, it can do no harm to reveal one trenchant fact, heretofore a guarded secret: three years ago, when the Duke and Duchess of Windsor suddenly reversed their decision to visit America, everyone wondered what had really occasioned that change of mind. It was simply that I had promised to act as their social guide on the trip, and then had to beg off, due to a slight misunderstanding with the law.

Perhaps my first real appreciation of the great truth of etiquette was born with an experience in Chillicothe, Ohio, in the fall of 1908. I was playing the old Onyx Theater. The headliner was a trained seal. His name was, I believe, Claude or Claudette. I won't swear to that—I have a poor memory for names; but I seldom remember a face.

This seal stayed with his trainer in an adjoining room to mine in the old Iroquois House. And it happened that one evening I returned to my room feeling uncommonly warm. So I entered the bath-between, intent on a refreshing tub. My friends, whom should I discover in the bathtub but Claude or Claudette (pardon my redundancy) sandwiched in between two twenty-pound cakes of ice.

"Unfortunate wretch," I mused, "having to be sealed in those hot furs on a day like this."

Despite my inner feelings, I spoke sharply—perhaps too sharply. I made it clear that I considered the whole

"I was playing the old Onyx Theater"

(Late 1890's)

incident an imposition, and then stalked back to my
bedroom in high dudgeon.

Presently I heard the ring of a buzzer from the bath-
between. I quickly ingurgitated a glass of cold ginger
ale in which I had placed some ice cubes and a mild
stimulant. A few moments after that, a considerable
sloshing of water was audible. I went to investigate.
And—on my word, friends—Claude or Claudette
(there I go again) had buzzed the desk for a brush and
was scrubbing the ring from the bathtub for me! Great
succulent, genuine tears streamed down my rosy cheeks,
passing my nose on both the left and right, dripping
from my chin onto a clean linen collar.

I never forgot that lesson. It taught me in a flash
what true etiquette is: *Consideration*. Consideration
for the other fellow.

I remember, years after the Claude or Claudette
episode, I was playing the old Star and Garter Theater
—it may have been just the Star—in Upper Wauke-
gan. It was bitter cold, snowdrifts fifteen feet high,
saloon doors frozen tight. I took deathly ill between the
afternoon and evening performances. There had been
a modest celebration of the trap drummer's birthday,
and I had evidently eaten a pretzel, or something, that
did not agree with me. I lay wretched on my hotel bed.
I could scarcely keep a mole on my stomach. I knew
that the inclement weather would keep attendance to
a minimum. But, nevertheless, I dragged myself to the
theater, literally staggering from lamppost to lamp-

post. When I got there, I found that there was *only one customer* out front.

"Friend," I said, "even though you alone are out

"It taught me in a flash what true etiquette is: Consideration. *Consideration for the other fellow."*

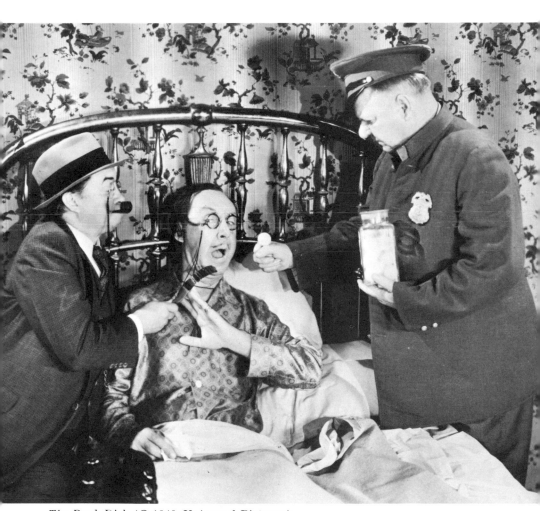

The Bank Dick (© 1940, Universal Pictures)

there to watch me, I assure you that I shall give my all, my full all. But may I first make your personal acquaintance?"

"Certainly," he said. "My name is Bush."

"I am honored. One of the Bush boys, I take it. And, as you doubtless know, my name is W. C. Fields."

He rose and stepped up on the stage. "Thanks," he said; "I just wanted to make sure you were him." And he served me with a subpoena.

"I am sorry," I told him, "that I have caused you to venture forth in this inclement weather. Had I known your office address, I should have called for it in person."

I wouldn't have been so bitter even at that, were it not that he didn't stay to see my act.

He had no consideration, my friends. No etiquette. Thorn Bush—that was his name—had not learned the lesson that Claude or Claudette had to teach mankind.

From experiences such as these, I have garnered finesse in every conceivable behavior situation. And this knowledge I pass on to my innumerable correspondents who write me daily, asking my counsel on the knottier problems of etiquette.

The limitations of space prevent me from covering more than a very few perplexing etiquette questions here. So I have selected a number of representative problems that confront every one of us in normal daily life:

The Glove-Recovering Emergency: Every night of

the year, approximately 700,000 American husbands suffer loss of time and physical indignity in peering under theater seats for their wives' gloves. I have devised a novel scheme that completely forestalls this social embarrassment. I have printed, 500 at a time, penny post cards reading: "Dear Manager: Tomorrow night my wife will attend your theater to lose a pair of gray suede gloves. You will greatly oblige by retrieving and sending same to address below." Mail these cards in good season, and I guarantee you a sixty-per-cent return.

The Elbows-on-Table Controversy: I agree with most other progressive social arbiters that placing the elbows on the dinner table is quite acceptable today. Putting the feet up is entirely another matter, however, and cannot be countenanced unless spats are worn.

The Large-Hat-in-Theater Menace: It is perfectly correct to lean forward and hiss in the offending lady's ear: "Madam, will you kindly remove that washbasket!" Give her thirty seconds, and if she does not respond, bring your cane down smartly on the top of her head. If you haven't a cane, an umbrella will do nicely.

The Mr. Mrrhrm Interlude: Many an otherwise scintillating party has been ruined by the host's having to introduce someone whose name he *should*, but does *not*, know. In this case, "dear old Frank or Johnny Mrrhrm" will generally get by if you cover up quickly by yelling across the room, "Hey, don't flick ashes in that goldfish bowl!"

"*Give her thirty seconds, and if she does not respond, bring your cane down smartly on top of her head.*"

"*Putting the feet up is entirely another matter, however, and cannot be countenanced unless spats are worn.*"

(© 1939, Universal Pictures)

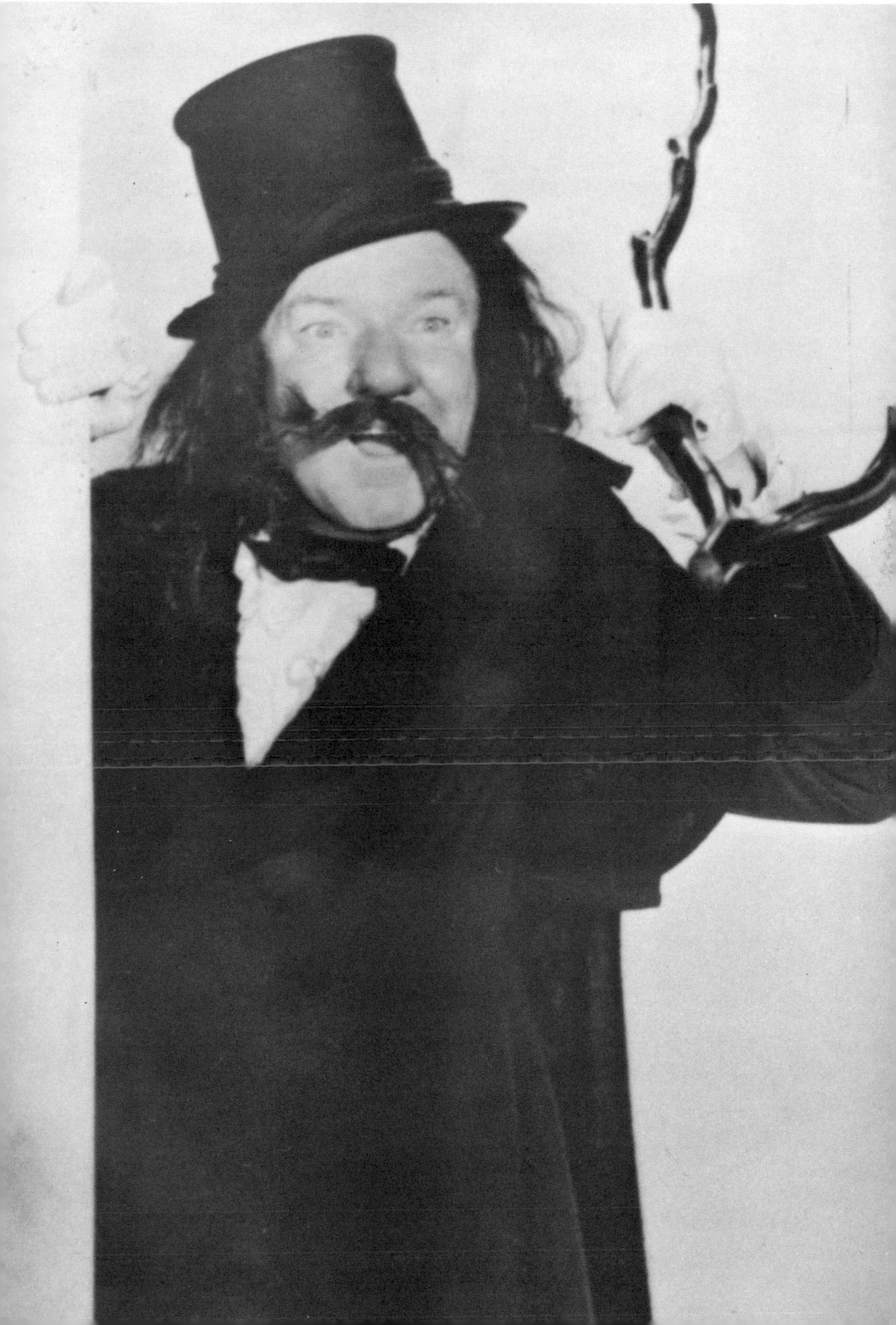

The Old Fashioned Way (© 1934, Paramount Pictures)

The Trolley-Car-Seating Problem: Various parts of the country feel differently about a gentleman's obligation to give up his seat to a lady in a trolley car. My solution is simple and merely calls for a practiced eye. I quickly estimate the weight of the bundles the lady is carrying. If over seventy pounds, I stand up—if I can stand up. Otherwise I fall forward.

The Listening-at-Keyhole Question: The practice of keyhole-listening is usually confined to hotels and boarding houses. It is absolutely indefensible to stoop so low. If the transom is not ajar, remember there are plenty of other rooms in the building.

The Recalcitrant-Slip Situation: What to do when a lady's slip shows in back is something that has never been satisfactorily decided. I, myself, prefer not to embarrass the victim by calling it to her attention. Rather, I always carry a special pair of shears for the emergency, with which I stealthily trim the slip even with the hem of the skirt. *Voilà*—no blush need burn my chickadee's fair face.

The Check-Grabbing Spectacle: Personally I have never been greatly troubled by this problem, being, as I am, the deliberate, slow-to-action type. However, for those who are continually embarrassed by the conventional squabble for the restaurant check, I'd advise this: When it comes to the point where, inevitably, the other person says, "Now, let's not fight about this," just answer, "Very well, old man." Remember, the complete gentleman never brawls.

The Voice-from-the-Back-Seat Hazard: This still constitutes the greatest single traffic menace in the United States. Manufacturers have marked up thirty years of rapid progress in the perfection of automobiles and accessories. How about spending a little time on the mass production of that exceedingly rare accessory —the little woman who can sit in the rear seat of a motor car without shouting, "Slow down, Harvey!"? I have only one method of procedure to recommend against the Voice from the Back Seat. When it shouts "Slow down," *slow down.* In fact, slow down to a complete stop, leap out of the car and thumb a ride back into town.

"I have only one method of procedure to recommend against the Voice from the Back Seat."

Never Give a Sucker an Even Break (© 1941, Universal Pictures)

Chapter **6**

How I Have Built Myself into a Physical Marvel

(© 1935, Paramount Pictures)

The great juggler managed to exercise regularly and kept himself in decent physical condition, although he refused to follow any but his own irregular training methods. He played an aggressive game of tennis and at golf shot respectably in the low 80's, but his workouts were little more than an excuse to build up his drinking arm. One of his favorite exercises was a mechanical rowing machine which he had installed in his home. Fields would place a martini on the bow of the vessel and row vigorously, seemingly in pursuit of the illusive prize. After about ten minutes he would halt his rowing, gulp the martini, and gleefully shout: "This is great exercise! It should increase my liquor capacity two or three hundred percent!"

"How I Have Built Myself into a Physical Marvel"

"Now, my muscles have been the wonder of two gen-erations and three continents."

(Late 1890's)

ALTHOUGH the demands on the Presidential physique have gradually been reduced to button-pushing (in order to open bridges, tunnels, or dams), still it is imperative to have a man in the White House who is as sound in body as he is in mind. Sounder, if possible—and it is possible.

Now, my muscles have been the wonder of two generations and three continents. Just to give you an example, I once had a twinge of rheumatism in my left arm and went to the doctor for a once-over. He inspected my arm, but could find nothing wrong. "Except," he said, "there is a strange little black speck on the muscle." I had to smirk! It was merely a tattoo—when I swelled my bicep it read, "Love from Mabel F. Cunningham."

However, like the late Teddy Roosevelt, I was not always the remarkable specimen I am today. In my youth I was distinctly frail. I well remember that many a time I could not even rush the can for Daddy in a proper manner. The two-quart container of beer was often more than a match for my slender young arm, and I would be forced to drink half the contents to make the burden lighter.

However, a curious thing happened to me while I was still but a swain; it changed my life. Here is the story in a nutshell:

It was just thirty-five years ago that I was talking to Tex Rickard and Death Valley Scotty in the Old Victoria Hotel Bar. I left the café and walked down Broadway. I must have been thinking, for the next thing I knew I was struck by a runaway street organ in Alleghany, Pa., and left in an unstrung condition. The entrepreneur of this musical cavalcade, an Italian gentleman, was most profuse in his apologies and sympathies. His poor frightened monkey bit me on the stomach in his excitement. As soon as I was out of the hospital, my thoughts turned to physical culture as a means of regaining my shattered health.

At the start of my health campaign I made one sad mistake, which should serve as a warning to my very dear readers not to rely on mechanical devices for exercise. I took $87.50 from my piggy bank and bought one of those rowing machines I'd heard so much about. Alas, the first time I put it in the Monongahela River and hopped on, the plagued thing sank like a plummet— am I using the right word? And I was bitten on the stomach in practically the same spot by a horn-billed turtle. When I arose to the surface and regurgitated a

"I took $87.50 from my piggy bank."

The Bank Dick (© 1940, Universal Pictures)

motley assortment of our diminutive finny friends and clay, my friends on the beach shouted, "Here's to you! Good luck! Bottoms up, you dumb—so and so," and things better left unsaid. They had evidently been drinking.

It was the Glad Gladiator who set me aright as to exercise and I shall never stop thanking the lucky co-incidence that brought his resonant voice to me. One very cold morning in March, I was wandering about the house trying to ferret out a noggin of medicinal spirits when my eye settled on the radio (radio was merely a chunk of crystal and a couple of earphones in those days). Fearing that my ears were about to chip with the cold, I donned the phones—and heard the Glad Gladiator broadcasting setting-up exercises. From that moment on, I was a slave to his vibrant "one-two-three—bend!" and every morning would find me at my deep-breathing, Grecian bends and crouching arabes-ques.

In time my muscles developed so that every time I lifted a glass the seams of my jacket would split. I was naturally grateful to the Glad Gladiator for my fine new physique, and one day I made my way to the radio station to view the great specimen of manhood with my own eyes. Unfortunately, I was told by the studio officials, the Glad Gladiator had only that morning dropped dead of pernicious anemia. My chin dropped, but then something happened that dried my tears. The studio's president, one Bela Nyiregyhazi, who knew

"I donned the phones—and heard the Glad Gladiator broadcasting setting-up exercises."

more about goulash than a seal does about swimming (these metaphors come to me as natural as—well, I can't think of one now), entered the room and spied me in the leopard skin I had slipped on for the occasion. "Give that beast a good currycombing and report tomorrow morning to take over for the Glad Gladiator," he said.

For a number of years I broadcast faithfully each morning, helping to build the bodies of America. The results gave me the greatest joy of my life. I received millions of wonderful letters of thanks, one of which I remember above all others. It was an epistle from Mrs. Smolen I. Sutker (whose husband at that time was a member of a group of Swiss bell-ringers who played at a famous restaurant) blessing me for saving her husband's life. Mr. Sutker, it seemed, could not sleep, for the noise made by disgruntled patrons calling him vile, ferocious and obscene names outside his window, so his good wife wrote to me begging for advice. I knew, of course, the great value of healthful recreation in such a case, so I advised him to run—which is healthful in more ways than one under the condition. I recently received a post card from him in a bottle. He is on one of the Coco Islands in the Pacific, perfectly happy exsept that a mosquito carried off his pet dog during one of his sleep periods.

On the other hand, I have known of instances where recreation did no good at all. Take my Uncle Oviatt MacTavish, a frugal old Scot. He became inflicted with insomnia so badly that his business was fast going to ruin. A friend suggested that he pitch horseshoes, and he tried it, but it didn't work. His horse got so sulky at having to go barefoot that Uncle Oviatt had to give up the sport and replace the shoes on the unfortunate equine.

But then, Uncle Sandy, as he was always referred to in the pawn-broking business, discovered an insomnia cure that earned him fame as the greatest sleeper south of Philadelphia. One day he happened to receive a free copy of the 1911 Congressional Record. On a warm Monday evening he sat down and read thirty pages. When he woke up it was Wednesday afternoon. He got so that after a good dose of the Congressional Record he could sleep as long as 192 hours on end. But his really crowning achievement came when he ran afoul of the law in 1916. It was a frame-up naturally, as you can guess. His enemies had planted a stolen overcoat on him.

I was standing beside him at the time he was apprehended to be placed in durance vile. We had gone to a café to celebrate my fifth year as a Thespian. An uncouth, ill-mannered lout rushed at me and ripped his gold-headed umbrella from my hand. (I had inadvertently picked it up, mistaking it for my cigar, as it was hanging on the bar beside it. The cigar and the umbrella handle being of the same hue, anyone can readily understand this mistake.) He struck me a violent blow just below the eye with a haymaker, raising

"He struck me a violent blow just below the eye with a haymaker . . ."

Trapeze (© 1935, Paramount Pictures)

an egg as big as a baby's fist on my cheek-bone, and said: "Take that, you ham!" "Ham and egg!" expostulated Uncle Sandy, laughing as though his ribs would burst.

But to revert to the overcoat episode: The judge sentenced Uncle Sandy to sixty days in jail. Uncle Sandy quietly stretched out on his bunk and slept through the whole term. And when they came to wake him up, he rolled over and asked for an extra sentence. I strongly doubt whether that record has ever been equaled even on the floor of the Senate.

Uncle Sandy lived to be 96, and he always claimed it was sleep that was responsible. But I am not sure that sleep *is* the most important thing in health. My Grandfather MacWeenie lived to be 104 and almost never went to bed. He attributed his longevity to his beard. It was the longest beard for hundreds of miles around, and Grandfather would wrap it around his neck like a muffler and stuff it down his trousers to keep his chest warm whilst crossing the moors during the grouse season. It functioned both as an adornment and combination underwear. Just to show you how long it was, one day Grandfather forgot to wrap it around his neck, and, while hurrying for a horse car, he missed his footing, ran right up his beard and kicked all his own teeth out—both of them.

One fall afternoon, Grandfather MacWeenie was forging his way through a Scotch mist down Suchiehall Street in Glasgow on his way to the House of Correction to see one of his relatives, when two flippant Yankees from New Orleans, U. S. A., passed. One of the Yankees looked first at Grandfather MacWeenie's splendid beard, then at his friend, the other Yankee, and sneered insultingly: "That muff would make great Winter quarters for bees and insects." Grandfather was dignified and paid them no mind—or he evidently didn't hear them, otherwise he possibly would have tried to sell them the beard.

At any rate, I am not a strong advocate of long beards and never have been.

I hope all my gentle readers will forgive my digression. As the exaggerated yarn goes with regard to the gentleman who jumped out the tenth-floor window and said when passing the sixth floor, "I've entirely gotten away from my story." As I was saying, I broadcast each morning for several years, and then one day I received a hard blow. Mr. Noel Whipsnade, our sponsor, came to me and said, "Fields, we're getting another Gladiator. You'll have to go. You're getting the well-known sack."

"But, Noel—" I said. He did not give me time to answer, even if I'd had one.

"At the last board meeting we decided radio was no longer in its infancy, Fields. It's the old laminster."

Of course, I could see his point, even though it left me stunned. But I was not to be discouraged. I then immediately embarked on a program of physical culture that was thrice—nay, four times—as hardy as

"I then immediately embarked on a program of physical culture that was thrice—nay, four times—as hardy as any I had undertaken before."

My Little Chickadee (© 1940, Universal Pictures)

any I had undertaken before. I would awake each morning at the crack of noon and walk a good three miles before breakfast to the old Rittenhouse Hostelry, for men only, where the newspaper boys hung out. Then came a long afternoon of baseball, where I learned to yell "Kill the umpire" louder than anyone else in the left-field bleachers. Then back to the boys at the old "Rit" as we succinctly (meaning briefly) referred to it. After dinner I would generally occupy myself with volley ball, sometimes varying that with a firemen's or policemen's ball. About midnight I would pick out a likely-looking table and catch forty winks under it. We had no patience with mollycoddles who slept in beds in those days. Soon I'd be back at my break-neck program, and would spend the rest of the night in figuring racing forms, and often as not I'd be able to pick up some fine tips from the bookies and stable hands. It only proves what methodical physical culture can do for you. Never, my gentle readers, take any stock in the man who says, "Pshaw, I sit at a desk all day and never do anything more strenuous than sign my name, and look at me —sound as a bell, sweet as a nut. Exercise is sheer bunkum!" How many times have I heard that twaddle! Little does the average business man know about himself. The truth is that he goes through more grueling calisthenics during a work day than the most active of coal heavers.

Take, for instance, Mr. Frothingham T. Whalebait, to choose a name at random from my morning mail.

Mr. Whalebait is third vice-president of a prosperous overshoe-buckle concern in Emporia, Kansas. The very first thing in the morning he executes one of the most advanced exercises I know of, called the *Triple Half-Nelson Twist:* when Mrs. W. calls him at eight A.M., he gets a head lock on the pillow, clutches the top of the bedclothing with one fist, contorts his whole body into a pretzel design and rolls over briskly on the inner-spring mattress. He reverses this figure at 8:05 when his wife shrieks again; and at 8:15 when she barges in at him with a jagged-edged broom, he pulls off his third Half-Nelson Twist and then gives up and gets dressed and takes a shower, time permitting.

The second exercise I have christened the *Coach-Window Adagio,* and it takes place after Mr. Whale-bait has caught the 8:57 by a hangnail and has finally found a seat. It consists of (a) grasping firmly both handles of a window; (b) exerting all the body pressure upwards; (c) invectives. After proper exhalation and subsequent inhalation of breath, Mr. W. repeats the exercise, and then decides to strangle for the remaining twenty minutes into town.

The third figure is executed after Mr. Whalebait has reached the office, and is called the *Sodium-Bicarbonate Dash:* at 9:45 he plunges to the elevator, then runs two blocks to the nearest drugstore.

The remainder of the morning Mr. Whalebait occupies himself with two minor, but healthful, exercises: the *Pencil-Sharpener Twirl* and the *Water-Cooler*

Sprint. The first he repeats until there are no pencils left in his desk; the latter until he feels everyone in the office will *know* he was partying the previous night.

Noontime is taken up by the *Cafeteria Shuffle,* a combination of holding both arms outstretched to support a tray and a practice session in broken-field running.

During the afternoon hours he devotes his energies almost exclusively to the *Executive Backstand,* consisting of tilting rearwards in a swivel chair to the angle of $45°$, lifting the legs slowly to the level of the desk, and placing the heels in true center of the glass desk-top. The sequence is rapidly reversed whenever there is a suspicious footstep just outside the office door.

Mr. Whalebait ends up a day of backbreaking exertion with the stiffest of all exercises, called the *Commuter's Cross-Country.* He begins this at 5:15 by raising the right arm and pressing the hand down firmly on the hat; crooking the left arm close to the abdomen, so as not to drop his briefcase, two pairs of three-thread hose that Mrs. W. requested him to pick up, four magazines, one newspaper, one detective novel from the lending library, one pair of roller skates for Junior, one box of cigars and an umbrella. After a brisk run down the platform, gaining a bit at every step on the train that is pulling out, he completes the exercise by performing a kind of running Eleanor Holm dive into the vestibule of the last car.

After such a program of physical culture, Mr. Whale-bait is in rousing good form for an evening of bridge. And yet he claims exercise plays no part in his life! Couldn't you kill such people? "Don't believe in exercise!"

And now, gentle readers, I wish to launch upon one important aspect of health which I have hitherto neglected. That is the matter of *diet*. Diet is ever so closely related to health, and the pity of it is that most of the so-called authorities are completely in error on the subject. Write to your Senators, tell them exactly what I told you and you can mention my name if you wish. Now, take the case of Mrs. F. Gordon Snavely. When Mrs. Snavely came to me she weighed 347 pounds without her stomacher and ear-rings—and had been dieting for seven years! She had been to Carlsbad, Vienna, Paris. She had gone to India where she ate curries and Bombay chutney with choice wines on the advice of Prince Ranje Manje of Umbey. She not only didn't lose any of her avoirdupois (fat) but gained a few pounds. She had gone to Budapest, where they had ordered lime juice and radishes for her; she had gone to Bucharest, where it had been celery tops and artichoke broth; she had gone to London, where it had been dreadfully rainy, as it always is in autumn months.

Finally she had returned to New York, and this is the diet they had concocted for her:

"Diet is ever so closely related to health, and the pity of it is that most of the so-called authorities are completely in error on the subject."

It's a Gift (© 1934, Paramount Pictures)

Breakfast

One crust of toast

¾ oz. gooseberry juice (strained)

Lunch

Small dandelion green

Acorn *au naturel*

Dinner

Eye-cup of iced tea (tepid with no sugar)

Three dried artichoke leaves (no sauce)

Moderate-sized finger bowl

Quite frankly I was shocked to find that she had gained eight pounds and now weighed 355 pounds. "See here, my little barn swallow," I admonished her in my fatherly way, "you have been going about this matter in entirely the wrong way. No wonder you were unable to get through the Holland Tunnel last Wednesday on your way to Perth Amboy to see your aunt." Thereupon I prescribed for her the Fields Fodder Fare for Fattened Femininity. Briefly this diet consists of the following: creamed pig's feet and mince pie for breakfast; double sirloin steak smothered in *pâté de fois gras* and two dozen buttered oysters for lunch; side of venison and a salad bowl of chocolate parfait for dinner; French pastry and beer between meals.

Whilst on this diet, I recommend the wearing of one of my diaphanous dresses for Dowager Duchesses which are selling like—for the lack of a better word—anything. These dresses are resilient and can be stretched like chewing gum. You first vaseline the body. Two

"I prescribed for her the Fields Fodder Fare for Fattened Femininity."

Never Give a Sucker an Even Break (© 1941, Universal Pictures)

jars come with each dress. You pull them over the head until exhausted. Then lie down. Repeat until relieved or satisfied. They come in three types. Slipon, pullon, and rayon, the latter by arrangement with Dupont de Nemours. These trade lasts are copyrighted, pirates beware, including the Scandinavian countries.

Well, my diet did the trick—and after only two months! When I visited Mrs. Snavely in the hospital she had dropped to 83 pounds and kept shrieking that she'd never touch another morsel of food as long as she lived. She smiled the last time I saw her and said: "Mr. F., you did this for me." It was a compliment I cherish. They were the last words she ever uttered. I sobbed like a child at her funeral. Her husband, to show his appreciation, gave me a Caboshon agate.

My success with Mrs. Snavely just goes to show that nothing is impossible. As a matter of fact, it was not even the first time in my life that I had achieved the impossible. In 1904, I was with Col. Catnip's Cat & Dog Circus doing an act. I followed the trained armadillos and my specialty was escaping from a straitjacket in two minutes flat. I'll never forget that afternoon in Medicine Hat—I was just starting my act when I heard a great hue and cry over by the lion cage. I cast a glance over my left shoulder—and there, charging down upon me, was a great, tawny, forest-bred lion.

Without even stopping to remove the strait-jacket, I leaped over four elephants. There was no applause for my colossal feat, as the audience had inadvertently

"In 1904 I was with Col. Catnip's Cat & Dog Circus doing an act."

The Ham Tree (circa 1906)

made their exit from the tent. But, nevertheless, it became a legend in Medicine Hat—how I did the impossible: leaped over four elephants in a strait-jacket.

And out of this experience comes the finest bit of health advice I could possibly give my dear readers: *Whenever a lion starts chasing you, don't stop to change your clothes.*

Chapter 7

The Care of Babies

"I, W. C. Fields, possess a deeper understanding of babies and their problems than any other statesman in America . . . I have made a life study of the dear little brats."

Never Give a Sucker an Even Break (© 1941, Universal Pictures)

Fields' attitude towards children is legendary. When asked "Do you like children?" he replied in his most endearing rasp, "I do if they're properly cooked!" To a group of admiring children he snarled, "You kids are disgusting, standing around here all day, reeking *of popcorn and lollipops!"*

During the filming of The Old Fashioned Way *(Paramount, 1934) he was called upon in one scene to be thoroughly and obnoxiously abused by Baby LeRoy, who dips Fields' watch in the gravy, twists his nose, and splatters a piece of pie over Fields' understanding face. Finally, when the others leave the room, and only Fields and LeRoy are left, Fields gets his revenge—and a true revenge it is! With the script originally calling for a gentle tap on the infant's upturned behind, Fields punted the unsuspecting child about fifteen feet across the room. After the scene, when questioned by the startled child's exasperated mother, Fields gloated, "I guess that will teach your precocious little brat not to try to steal scenes from me!"*

"I always carried a number of sterilized blindfolds, which I would casually place over each baby's eyes before I kissed it."

Tilly and Gus (© 1933, Paramount Pictures)

THE FUTURE of our country lies solely in the babies of today (God help them) and they certainly deserve the first and last consideration of any Presidential candidate. I do not hesitate to state that I, W. C. Fields, possess a deeper understanding of babies and their problems than any other statesman in America. For, over and above the fact that I was once a baby myself, I have made a life study of the dear little brats. And my work has not gone unnoticed by the public. Just consider the number of children that have been named for me—why, there must be close to a million Williams in the United States alone.

To give you an example of my comprehension of infant psychology, on my last swing around the corn-belt states, I always carried a number of sterilized blindfolds, which I would casually place over each baby's eyes before I kissed it. This prevented its growth from being stunted through terror.

It was more than any other candidate was willing to do for American babyhood, and, believe me, the parents of the nation appreciated my thoughtfulness.

Rarely a day passes that I do not receive letters from anxious mothers soliciting my advice and counsel on the care of their nippers. Only last Sunday morning I was reading one of these pathetic missives as I trudged down to the cellar in search of a eucalyptus log (I always keep a supply of these on hand in case I contract a dry throat).

The letter was from one Mrs. G. Waldo Pearlfender and it read, in part: "What can we do with our three-year-old Junior? He becomes positively violent whenever we try to give him a bath."

It was an interesting coincidence that just at the moment I was reading those lines my gaze fell on an old washing machine—ball-bearing with a rubber crank—which I bought for Mrs. Fields as a wedding present. It is outmoded now, but it was considered a whiz in its day. Mrs. F. was very proud of it and often sobbed audibly with sentiment as she heaved at the crank.

But, gentle readers, the point is that the moment I viewed that noble engine, I knew what I would write to Mrs. Pearlfender. "My *dear* Mrs. P.," I would caution her, "due to an unfortunate experience of my own, I have come to the conclusion that bathing children too often is apt to be extremely dangerous."

Only too well do I remember the abovementioned

incident. It occurred when my nephew Kermit came to live with us twenty years ago. During the first month we tried to put the little fellow in the bathtub twice. Once he stuck his baby foot down my throat and, on another occasion, in my eye. Ultimately Mrs. F. and myself seized him unawares and emptied him into the washing machine. Mrs. F. then fell to at the crank, and little Kermit bounded about in the vat with a heart-warming rattle. We repeated this treatment several times with good results. Alas, one day while Mrs. F. was doing yeoman's work at the crank, I was called away to the telephone and forgot to tell her when to stop. Half an hour later I descended to the cellar—and she was still cranking. "Halt!" I cried, and snatched the cover off the vat. Too late! The soapy water had shrunk Kermit to the size of my grandfather's beaver hat. If I had not had the presence of mind to run him hastily through the wringer, thereby bringing him back to his normal height, he might have spent the rest of his life as a midget with the circus. As it is, poor Kermit is still only a shell of his former self.

Over and above that experience, I thought of my own father's deep distrust of water. In Daddy's time there were many normal citizens who thought water a pleasant refreshment, never dreaming of its diabolical effects. Papa in '78 journeyed up the River of Doubt with a party of explorers headed by the then-eminent Dr. Hugo Phirst. One afternoon their boat capsized and their supply of medicinal spirits floated down to the

"The soapy water had shrunk Kermit to the size of my grandfather's beaver hat."

My Little Chickadee (© 1940, Universal Pictures)

mouth of the turbulent, cayman-infested stream. Thenceforth poor Father was compelled to rely on water—for the first time in fifty years. He contracted yellow fever as a result, and though he was not the type to say, "I told you so," he was very cross about the whole incident.

In the light of both these unfortunate experiences, I finally concluded that a program of *moderation* was what Mrs. Pearlfender needed. There should be a board of mediation set up, consisting of, say, a senator, a jurist and an industrial head—all of whom must be men both Junior and Mrs. P. trusted implicitly—and that board should decide just when Junior was to be dunked and how often.

I must acknowledge that the inspiration for this brilliant plan of mine came directly from Mr. John L. Lewis's N. L. R. B., the miraculous success of which has left us all a little dazed. It has long been a mystery to me why the present incumbent of the White House, Franklin D. Roosevelt, doesn't form such a board of moderators for himself.

Indeed, moderation is my middle name (though I do not often use it in signing legal documents). The value of moderation I learned from my very wise mother when I myself was but a tot. I was a restless little fellow, possessed of a lusty mezzo-soprano larynx. At twelve-thirty each night I was wont to make the frame of "Bless Our Happy Home" tremble on the wall. At such times my good mother would wake and carry me to and fro about the nursery. After a half-hour of this she would cry out exhaustedly to my father, "John, *you* come and carry the thing!" One warm night in July I was in particularly good voice, and my mother carried me for a good three-quarters of an hour. Then she gasped to my father, "John, *you* carry the thing!" Father came and carried me violently all over the house for over an hour. Finally, with a scream of despair, he carried me right out of the house and down to Joe's Place where he washed down some potato chips with a glass of cheer. I can still remember the stern but self-composed look on my mother's face as she swept majestically into that barroom after Father. She looked straight into his eye. "John," she said evenly, "this is what I call carrying the thing too far."

While still phrasing my answer to Mrs. P. in my mind, I found a suitable eucalyptus log and started for the stairs. My eye lit once more on the trusty washing machine, and I speculated sadly on the fact that the women of today must dress and taxi to gymnasium clubs for their exercise. There they must content themselves with a rowing machine, or tossing a medicine ball, which is much heavier than a washbasket, and more awkward, having no handles.

I was just about to mount the stairs when the doorbell rang violently. It gave me such a start that I ascended the stairs three to five at a time—in my excitement I forgot to count the exact number. Suffice to say that when I opened the front door, there before me stood

Mrs. Neville Pratt, a friend of long standing. She had run down hastily from a near-by nudist camp without even stopping to comb her hair.

"Godfrey Daniel! What brings you here?" I cried. "Aren't you cold without your gloves?" I invited her into my tastefully arranged sitting room and sat her down on our horse-hair sofa. I stood silent as she gazed blankly at the opposite wall, where hung a stuffed giant sardine under glass, bagged by a distant relative of my family, and a tapestry that pictured two well-fed beagle hounds, one with a pheasant in his mouth and the other just staring off in the general direction of the umbrella stand.

"Come, speak!" I said, admiring her artistic long fingers, meticulously groomed.

"I suppose you wonder why I came to you at this unearthly hour?" she whispered hoarsely.

She had me flummoxed. Does she want to borrow the lawn mower? I asked myself.

She spoke again: "It is about our little Nathaniel. Last Wednesday we had the brace taken off his teeth, and he has wept bitterly ever since. What, Mr. Fields, oh, *what* are we to do?"

"Madam!" I cried, deeply shocked. "Do you mean to tell me you have *no* comprehension of the child mind? Without his brace he feels positively undressed!"

You see, my friends, it takes only a little discernment to solve the problems of youth. Understanding that comes of a willingness to enter into their thoughts and

"...it takes only a little discernment to solve the problems of youth. Understanding that comes of a willingness to enter into their thoughts and feelings—even into their games."

(© 1941, Universal Pictures)

feelings—even into their games. Nothing could illustrate this better than an experience of my own several
years ago. During a very hot August I was entrusted
with the care of my little godson Nesbit, and every day
without fail I would take him for a stroll in an impro-
vised carriage made from a soapbox, the sides of which
were emblazoned with a well-known manufacturer's
name.

One especially warm afternoon I placed Nesbit in
the soapbox and wheeled him down to the neighborhood tobacconist. As we approached the gutter on the
far side of the street, I doffed my hat to a young lady
whom I felt sure I knew. My heel caught on an Ecua-
dorian banana peel. I lurched forward, bearing down
on the handle of the makeshift gocart. Little Nesbit
catapulted into the air and I toppled face-first into his
perambulator.

A precipitous hill was before me; I was in a desperate
situation. It called for calm nerves and grit. As a boy I
was nicknamed "Gritty" by my playmates. As I bumped
wildly over the cobblestones I noticed many little boys
plunging downhill in contraptions similar to mine. Suddenly a strong breeze whisked my white derby hat into
the middle of the street. A horse stepped on it. I was
bereft of the last vestige of dignity.

Upon my arrival at the bottom of the hill a gentleman with a flag raised my right hand, patted me on the
back and shouted, "The winner of the Soapbox Derby!"
I said, "This is a soapbox, all right, but I've lost my

"I placed Nesbit in the soapbox and wheeled him down to the neighborhood tobacconist."

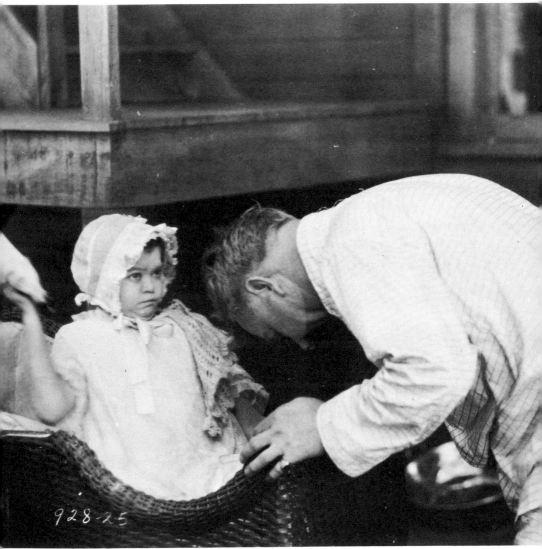

The Old Army Game (Famous Players-Lasky Corp., 1926)

derby." The crowd roared with laughter and applauded the clever rejoinder for fully fifteen minutes. Newspaper photographers were flashing bulbs all about me. Women tossed jewelry. Then another official stalked to the fore and rasped, "This little rosy-nosed lad looks more than five to me." So subsequently I was disqualified as being overage (I still think I might have gotten away with it had I had the presence of mind to ditch my cigar). But the resultant publicity made a deep impression on the housewives all over the nation. They realized I was a man who understood the child mind, who could enter into their world with perfect understanding.

That is why, as I previously stated, rarely a day passes that I do not receive letters from busy mothers asking me to take care of their babies for them, offering the union rate of forty cents an hour.

Naturally it would be impossible for a busy man like myself to interrupt my researches at the neighborhood race track for even one afternoon, so into each reply envelope I slip a brief compendium of hints dealing with the most troublesome problems on bringing up children. I regard it as my masterpiece, and out of pure bigness of heart I reprint a bit of it herewith for the benefit of each and every one of my gentle readers.

EXCERPTS FROM THE FIELDS PLAN (SERIES D)

Problem of Diet: A child should never be given pig's knuckles or corn on the cob until the first little toofums have appeared.

Problem of Sleep: Until a tot is at least three, it should be packed off to bed by midnight, even though the party may be just getting really started. It should be warmly covered and have plenty of fresh air. I hesitate, however, to advise that a child sleep outdoors. I tried this practice several times myself but never got a decent night's sleep—policemen were forever waking me up and cautioning me to git goin'.

Problem of Christmas: When a lad is about eight he is apt to become quarrelsome on Christmas Day and insist on playing with his new electric trains. Fathers should be very firm in such cases, asking the boy or girl who he thinks paid for the trains anyway—Santa Claus? (Young ladies have taken me for Santa on so many occasions I'm beginning to hate the name.)

Problem of Education: It is important for boy children, at least, to learn to count money at the age of four, since it is high time that they were out selling papers. If small for its age, the child can sell tabloids.

Problem of Difficult Questions: As a child grows from infancy to adolescence it will, from time to time, belabor you with a series of baffling questions. To lessen the burden on the American parent, I pick three of the knottiest questions and supply Fields-tested, foolproof replies.

1. Question (occurring at the age of four, about two a.m. in the morning): "Daddy, can I have a glass of water?"

Answer: "Certainly, sonny boy, if you'll bring me one, too."

2. Question (age ten): "Daddy, why were you kissing the maid last night?"

Answer: "It's a tarradiddle—a fib! Besides, she mistook me for the plumber."

3. Question (age eighteen, the day before the big football game): DEAR GOVERNOR STOP AM STRAPPED STOP CAN YOU WIRE TWENTY DOLLARS?

Answer: NO STOP MALE PARENT.

David Copperfield (© Metro-Goldwyn-Mayer Inc. 1935)

"Question: 'Daddy, why were you kissing the maid last night? Answer: 'It's a tarradiddle—a fib!'"

Chapter 8

How to Succeed in Business

My Little Chickadee (© 1940, Universal Pictures)

Most interesting of Fields' business practices was his outrageous system of banking. He made it a habit to open an account in most of the large cities he visited, and he often opened them under assumed names (Mahata Kane Jeeves, Otis Criblecoblis, etc.). Whether he did this to hide his money from greedy relatives or from the government, or just to assure himself that getaway money was always nearby was never entirely clear. For whatever the reasons, his system was quite novel.

Once in 1944 a friend questioned him on his procedures while examining a few dozen of his hundreds of bank books. Fields confided that he even had about $50,000 spread around war infested Germany. "But why?" inquired the astonished friend. "In case that little bastard wins!" gargled the crafty Fields.

"How to Succeed in Business"

ANY OF US who are over twelve years of age—and a great many of us *are* over twelve years of age—must surely remember the fateful year of 1929. Many world-shaking events took place in 1929, including Mrs. Gann's great White House victory, and Mrs. Gene Tunney's appendectomy. Also, Shirley Temple was born and Clyde Van Deusen won the Kentucky Derby.

Of course these memorable happenings are imprinted indelibly in the minds of all Americans. But one other important thing occurred in October of 1929 that was barely noticed at the time and has been all but forgotten since. I refer to certain irregularities in some of Wall Street's finest stocks.

Now, about a week after this curious mishap—one witty city editor dubbed it "The Crash"—I was dining with several of the nation's greatest financial wizards at the Automat. We were all in a pensive mood, and in the course of conversation the president of a vast department-store chain addressed me. "Mr. Fields," he asked, fumbling in his pockets for an after-dinner cigar butt, "what in your mind has occasioned the recent upset in the market?"

"Gentlemen," I began, in a stern but not unkind tone, "the whole trouble is a simple and fundamental one: briefly, you have tried to sell the American people more than they could pay for."

Each of the moguls nodded their gray pates abashedly.

"I could have told you several years ago," I continued, "that you were heading for this catastrophe. Let me recount an ingenuous little anecdote to illustrate the point. It all began twenty years ago when I first learned the fundamental rule of business success from one of the most astute economics experts who ever trod this green earth. He was a homespun geologist by the name of Doctor George T. Spelvin, and he had amassed a goodly fortune from the sale of several dozen oil wells situated in the middle of the Great Salt Lake. His crude but sound success formula was as follows, stated in his quaint Yankee dialect:

1. Find out how much they gut.
2. Git it.
3. Git!

"In the course of my very first business venture,

gentlemen, I learned how very true old Doctor Spelvin's philosophy was. I took a flyer in vacuum-cleaner selling, and on my initial day of canvassing I came

---

". . . he had amassed a goodly fortune from the sale of several dozen oil wells situated in the middle of the Great Salt Lake."

The Old Fashioned Way (© 1934, Paramount Pictures)

across a household that looked like a capital prospect, for through the window I could see a lady busy cleaning the living-room carpet with an old-fashioned carpet sweeper. I knocked at the front door and introduced myself with my never-failing gallantry. The lady seemed skeptical—said not a word. 'Madam,' I said, 'allow me to demonstrate this miraculous contrivance.' Whereupon I brought the vacuum cleaner in and fell to work upon the living room. I toiled over that carpet until it was clean enough to eat off—though a regular table would have been more comfortable, I'll admit. The lady, however, merely stared.

"My stick-to-it-iveness asserted itself and I spent another half hour on the dining-room rug. Still there was no word of approval forthcoming. Determined not to lose a possible sale, I carried the apparatus upstairs and spent the rest of the morning on the bedroom rugs. But silence still greeted my efforts.

"Finally I lost patience. 'Madam,' I gasped, 'will you tell me one thing—are you or are you not interested in purchasing this machine?'

"'Well, mister,' she replied, 'you'll have to wait til the missus gets home—I only came in to clean.'"

Upon the conclusion of my tale, several of the tycoons drew out their handkerchiefs and wept a little. It was a moving sight. "How true," they whispered. "How very true! Fields, if we had only understood this great principle before. . . ."

Of course it was inevitable that my advice fell on

"I knocked at the front door and introduced myself with my never-failing gallantry."

Tilly and Gus (© 1933, Paramount Pictures)

deaf ears in one case. He was a motorcar mogul, and several years after the Automat episode, he defied my stated fundamentals by okaying automobile sales to 5,000 purchasers whom he believed to be W. P. A. workers. It turned out that they were only ordinary job holders and could not meet the payments.

But let us get down to the more definite problems of the moment. For instance, how should the young man just out of college go about insuring himself of a successful career in the present-day business world?

That is a big question, and one not easy to answer— even for an expert of my caliber. However, I would say that the young man's first step should be the choice of a suitable occupation. From my wide observation of the matter, I would counsel him to eschew the more common fields of endeavor and try his luck in one that is uncrowded. Just for instance, there is great room for expansion in the truffle industry today. Verily, it is crying out for young blood. The truffle industry is divided into four phases:

1. Raising the truffles
2. Training pigs to rout out the truffles
3. Packing the truffles
4. Manufacturing old kit bags to pack the truffles in

But there are many other neglected fields that offer just as fine opportunities as the truffle industry, among which are the manufacture of magic-lantern slides,

"... *how should the young man just out of college go about insuring himself of a successful career in the present-day business world?*"

Sally of the Sawdust (© 1925, United Artists)

carriage-wheel striping, designing paper panties for lamb chops, ice-cream-cone embossing and castanet tuning.

When the young man has finally chosen what his life work shall be, the next important problem is how to approach a prospective employer. At this point I should like to offer a few valuable hints pertaining to the actual application for employment.

1. Never show up for an interview in bare feet.

2. Do not read your prospective employer's mail while he is questioning you as to qualifications.

3. Remember to have no liquor bottles visible on your person; but if you *should* forget, at least have the decency to offer your prospective employer a pull.

After the young man has finally landed a job in his chosen field of endeavor he must make up his mind on one important score, namely, that there is only one way to rise to the top of the heap in any occupation or profession, be it humble or lofty: you must give it your all; you must do a little bit more than is expected of you. For instance, young man, you may be only an elevator operator—but if a customer wants to go to the eighth floor, take him to the ninth or tenth. The small extra effort may prove the turning point in your career. The same principle is true in the more glorified professions: if you are a politician, spurn the opportunities for petty graft here and there—try to get a post

"Remember to have no liquor bottles visible on your person; but if you should forget, at least have the decency to offer your prospective employer a pull."

Never Give a Sucker an Even Break (© 1941, Universal Pictures)

on some New Deal agency where there's real money.

In short, model your life after Old Tom, who gave his very life for the furtherance of his profession's ideals.

Possibly you do not know the story of Old Tom? Well, I will tell it to you—and a most remarkable story it is, too. Old Tom was the only common house fly who ever received a degree from Harvard Medical School. Of course, there were many flies who hung around the laboratories for short periods, but Old Tom was the only one earnest enough to work through the whole curriculum.

Strangely enough, upon graduation, Old Tom became inoculated with the desire for adventure, despite his primary interest in medicine. And this is how I come to know his history so well. You see, my granduncle Daldo B. Daldo was the proprietor of a thriving flea circus at the time, and glamour-hungry Old Tom joined his troupe, where he soon became a star specialty act.

Shortly afterwards Granduncle Daldo succumbed from injuries sustained in a friendly game of cards (one of the players evidently mistook him for someone else and shot him). He left my Grandaunt Fancy Dalbo, his wife, a three-quarters interest in the world-famed Old Tom, which, after considerable litigation with relatives, she disposed of to Professor Hymie Schickelgruber, a fly trainer of renown in those days.

At the zenith of his career, Old Tom was the toast of the fair sex as well as the foul. He was seen nightly in both high spots and low spots. Tom learned to love the

Professor, and the Professor looked upon Tom as his own child. Other flies grew to know and love the Professor too. They gathered about him in hordes.

One night at a swanky night spot around 135th Street, a smartly-dressed young lady passed the Professor's table. He doffed his velour hat and smiled coyly. He mistook her for a girl he had met in Johannesburg, or perhaps Rhodesia. She rebuffed his seeming familiarity with a flippant "Amscray, bum, you draw flies!" This he accepted as a fervent compliment. He clicked his heels and, bowing graciously, backed over a cuspidor and struck his head on the brass footrail, much to the amusement of the uncouth, although beautiful, young lady.

But to revert to Old Tom—for an account of one of his most exciting adventures, read Professor Hemmendinger's article in *Die Mitwoch Zeitung* of January 29, 1876, Dusseldorf (try to get the *Abend* green flash edition; they are rather scarce).

Professor Hemmendinger—associated with flies and fly circuses for over thirty years—describes one of the bloodiest battles he ever witnessed between Tom and a renegade fly, a real toughie, who had crawled in through an opening in the screen to the fly circus. Seven fly cops with much difficulty and loss of blood managed to quell the excitement and stop the battle after Old Tom had vanquished his rough, loud-mouthed adversary.

Professor Hemmendinger traced the cause of the

"Professor Hemmendinger—associated with flies and fly circuses for over thirty years—"

Two Flaming Youths (© 1927, Paramount Pictures)

fight to certain names which the intruder flung at Old Tom. (The Professor spent much of his time standing, sitting or lying around in saloons listening to bar flies. He recognized and translated twenty-seven distinct fly dialects.) He claims that the renegade referred to Old Tom as a "horse fly, a plant louse, you Diptera Muscidae, you Hymenoptera, you low ichneumon fly." Tom, of course, was a Musca domestica. He had lived with the Morgans and the Vanderbilts. Naturally, he could not brook such insults.

Tom was strong and handsome in those days. He ran his clean, powerful hind limbs back over his sturdy body, sleeking his wings and stroking his head with vigorous determination. Then, hissing between his teeth, he leaped clear over a lead pencil and attacked his adversary. It called for quiet nerves, a level head and grit, and if ever a fly had these attributes, it was Old Tom. He was like Orson Welles in that respect and yet in other ways resembled Sumner.

There was a great fluttering of wings in the fly arena. Flies flew in every direction. It seemed imminent that an accident in midair would occur and at least a couple of flies would crash to earth.

While it lasted, the fight was a spectacle of unforgettable drama. It's a shame that Henri Ferber could not have witnessed it as a sports writer.

Soon after the battle Old Tom's adventurous spirit reasserted itself and he went to live in an old boarding house in the Bowery. There he met an English relative named Cecil, a famous fly in his own right, whose grandfather had been the original fly in the ointment. Tom and Cecil would crawl on the ceiling at night while Cecil painted alluring pictures of Liverpool and its drays and lorries and Percheron horses.

Tom dreamed of Percheron horses for several weeks and then decided to beat his way to Liverpool on a cattle boat. Once he got there, he lived for some time at the old Langehanke Delicatessen and Beer Shop on Lime Street. Tiring of the humdrum life and the continual rains, he joined three tsetse flies and embarked on a sailing vessel for Zomba, Africa, where he led an attack on a group of German explorers.

Eventually he was caught by the Earl of Swafham on the Zambezi River, who, not knowing that Tom was an English sympathizer, placed him on a hook as fish bait—but he escaped. Crippled by this cruel and humiliating experience, he returned to England on a private yacht, and started life anew by working as a model for a fish-fly manufacturing concern at Stoke Poges. Later he took up quarters with the Lord of Epping Forest and followed His Lordship to his ducal castle in Scotland, where he became such a favorite that he was permitted to indulge not wisely but too well on sugar. He soon developed Bright's Disease. And here is where Old Tom's great professional heroism comes in; it should stand as a beacon light for every young man and woman embarking on a career. Follow me closely, now:

When Lord Epping discovered Tom's ailment he

hastily summoned a Harley Street physician. The great doctor, whose name I do not care to mention for ethical reasons, donned his greatcoat, galoshes and umbrella and rushed posthaste to St. Pancras Station. He was making the trip against his better judgment, since a serious epidemic of ingrowing toenail was raging in London, and his services were sorely needed. However, when his train reached Rugby the conductor shouted, "Telegram for Dr. Effingham!" (I'm sorry that I'm now compelled to reveal the doctor's name.) Dr. Effingham accepted the telegram and said, "That will be all, thank you," and gave the fellow tuppence. Then he slit the telegram and read of Tom's death!

The real story behind the tragedy is this: Tom had learned of Lord Epping's summons to Dr. Effingham, and realized that there was not one chance in a hundred for recovery. So, with the words of the Hippocratic Oath on his drawn, pale lips, he leaped off a shelf onto a strip of fly paper. Yes, Old Tom committed insecticide! But it was for the furtherance of the profession's ideals: he knew that this was the only way to turn Dr. Effingham back to London, where his incredible skill might stem the crushing epidemic.

I am happy to report that Old Tom's beautiful sacrifice was not in vain. Dr. Effingham, after reading the telegram, opened his great portmanteau and removed a full quart of a well-known brand manufactured in the North. He took several swigs. Some careless person had left the window of his compartment open, and the doctor fell out, landing upon the engine bumper of a south-bound express. He arrived back at Waterloo Station in time for his morning practice.

R. I. P., Old Tom. I never knew a fly with higher ideals!

But now, to get back to the stark, work-a-day aspect of life: I feel sure that at this point thousands of my readers are saying to themselves, "It's all very fine for Mr. Fields to go on about the ideals of business, but with conditions as they are today, it looks very much as though the nation won't have any business to be idealistic about pretty soon. What is Mr. Fields going to do about that?"

My friends, it is a wise and justifiable question. And I, as a candidate for the highest office in this fair land, will tell you straight from the shoulder exactly what I intend to do to put business back on its feet. My plan is simplicity itself.

In the first place, just what is wrong with business today? Ask any expert and he will tell you that business suffers from two distinct ailments:

1. Overtaxation
2. Labor unrest, strikes, picketing, etc.

Well, the solution ought to be plain to anyone. There are 50,000,000 workers and 10,000,000 unemployed. Merely remove all taxation from business and stipulate

"...*with conditions as they are today, it looks very much as though the nation won't have any business to be idealistic about pretty soon. What is Mr. Fields going to do about that?*"

(© 1940, Universal Pictures)

that employers must spend this great saving in hiring pickets—one picket for every five workers they employ. Presto, no more taxes, no more unemployed, no more labor unrest—everybody happy!

This is the platform that W. C. Fields, "The Friend of the People," stands firm upon, and I dare F. D. R. himself to think up a scheme that sounds half as good.

Remember, folks, cast a vote for Fields and watch for the silver lining. Cast several votes for Fields and watch for the police.

"Remember, folks, cast a vote for Fields and watch for the silver lining. Cast several votes for Fields and watch for the police."

The Old Fashioned Way (© 1934, Paramount Pictures)